ECONOMIC ISSUES, PROBLEMS AND PERSPECTIVES

THE FEDERAL RESERVE

OVERSIGHT AND TRANSPARENCY

ECONOMIC ISSUES, PROBLEMS AND PERSPECTIVES

Additional books in this series can be found on Nova's website under the Series tab.

Additional E-books in this series can be found on Nova's website under the e-books tab.

MONETARY, FISCAL AND TRADE POLICIES

Additional books in this series can be found on Nova's website under the Series tab.

Additional E-books in this series can be found on Nova's website under the e-books tab.

ECONOMIC ISSUES, PROBLEMS AND PERSPECTIVES

THE FEDERAL RESERVE

OVERSIGHT AND TRANSPARENCY

GERRIE R. CONLEY
AND
ADOLF A. SANFORD
EDITORS

Nova Science Publishers, Inc.
New York

For permission to use material from this book please contact us:
Telephone 631-231-7269; Fax 631-231-8175
Web Site: http://www.novapublishers.com

LIBRARY OF CONGRESS CATALOGING-IN-PUBLICATION DATA

ISBN: 978-1-62081-034-7

Published by Nova Science Publishers, Inc. † New York

CONTENTS

PREFACE

Critics of the Federal Reserve (Fed) have long argued for more oversight, transparency, and disclosure. Criticism intensified following the extensive assistance provided by the Fed during the financial crisis. More specifically, critics have focused on the Government Accountability Office (GAO) audits of the Fed and the disclosure of details on the identities of borrowers and the terms of those loans. This book examines oversight and disclosure issues relating to the Federal Reserve with a focus on the Dodd-Frank Wall Street Reform and Consumer Protection Act; QE 3; and Federal Reserve transparency.

Chapter 1 - Congress has delegated monetary policy duties to the Federal Reserve (Fed), but retains oversight responsibilities. The Fed enjoys an unusual degree of independence from Congress and the president compared to other government agencies. Proponents of these arrangements argue that this independence results in good, non-political policymaking and a high degree of credibility with financial markets. Critics of the Fed argue that it performs essential government functions, yet is more opaque and unaccountable than other government agencies. Following the financial crisis, they assailed the Fed's decision to extend more than $1 trillion of assistance to the financial sector—exceeding the amount extended by the Troubled Asset Relief Program (TARP)—without any congressional input. These critics call for more oversight, transparency, and disclosure for the Fed. More specifically, critics have focused on the Government Accountability Office (GAO) audits of the Fed and the disclosure of details on the identities of borrowers and terms of loans.

Chapter 2 - Events surrounding the 2007 financial crisis raised questions about the governance of the 12 Federal Reserve Banks (Reserve Banks), particularly the boards of directors' roles in activities related to supervision and regulation. The Dodd-Frank Wall Street Reform and Consumer Protection Act required GAO to review the governance of the Reserve Banks. This report (1) analyzes the level of diversity on the boards of directors and assesses the extent to which the process of identifying possible directors and appointing them results in diversity on the boards, (2) evaluates the effectiveness of policies and practices for identifying and managing conflicts of interest for Reserve Bank directors, and (3) compares Reserve Bank governance practices with the practices of selected organizations. To conduct this work, GAO reviewed bylaws, policies, and board minutes for each Reserve Bank, conducted a survey of directors who served in 2010, reviewed governance policies at comparable institutions, and interviewed officials from the Board of Governors of the Federal Reserve System (Federal Reserve Board) and Reserve Banks, directors from each bank, and selected academics.

Chapter 3 - Thank you Chairman Ron Paul, Ranking Member William Lacy Clay and members of the subcommittee for this opportunity to testify on transparency at the Federal Reserve. My name is Robert Auerbach. I am a Professor of Public Policy at the Lyndon B. Johnson School of Public Affairs at the University of Texas in Austin. On two separate occasions I had the honor to serve as an economist on the staff of this committee (1977-81 and 1992-1997) and my 2008 book, Deception and Abuse at the Fed: Henry B. Gonzalez Battles Alan Greenspan"s Bank details the oversight investigations that I staffed while serving Committee Chairman Henry S. Reuss in the late 1970's and Committee Chairman/Ranking Member Henry B. Gonzalez in the 1990's. I have also served as an economist in the U.S. Treasury's Office of Domestic Monetary Affairs during the Reagan administration and at the Federal Reserve System.

Chapter 4 - Chairman Paul, Ranking Member Clay, and distinguished members of the subcommittee, I thank you for the invitation to appear at today's important hearing. I am Mark Calabria, Director of Financial Regulation Studies at the Cato Institute, a nonprofit, non-partisan public policy research institute located here in Washington, DC. Before I begin my testimony, I would like to make clear that my comments are solely my own and do not represent any official policy positions of the Cato Institute. In addition, outside of my interest as a citizen and taxpayer, I have no direct financial interest in the subject matter before the Committee today, nor do I represent any entities that do.

In: The Federal Reserve ISBN: 978-1-62081-034-7
Editors: G. R. Conley and A. A. Sanford© 2012 Nova Science Publishers, Inc.

Chapter 1

Federal Reserve: Oversight and Disclosure Issues*

Marc Labonte

Summary

Critics of the Federal Reserve (Fed) have long argued for more oversight, transparency, and disclosure. Criticism intensified following the extensive assistance provided by the Fed during the financial crisis. More specifically, critics have focused on the Government Accountability Office (GAO) audits of the Fed and the disclosure of details on the identities of borrowers and the terms of those loans.

Some critics downplay the degree of Fed oversight and disclosure that already takes place. For oversight, the Fed has been required by statute to report to and testify before the House and Senate committees of jurisdiction semi-annually since 1978. In addition, these committees periodically hold more focused hearings on Fed topics. Contrary to popular belief, GAO has conducted frequent audits of the Fed since 1978, subject to statutory restrictions. In addition, the Fed's financial statements are audited by private sector auditors. The Dodd-Frank Act (P.L. 111-203) resulted in an audit of the Fed's emergency activities during the financial crisis, released in July 2011, and an audit of Fed governance, released in October 2011. The effective result of the audit restrictions

* This is an edited, reformatted and augmented version of a Congressional Research Service publication, CRS Report for Congress R42079, from www.crs.gov, prepared for Members and Committees of Congress, dated November 10, 2011.

remaining in law is that GAO cannot evaluate the economic merits of Fed policy decisions. In the 112th Congress, H.R. 459, H.R. 1496, and S. 202 would remove all statutory restrictions on GAO audits.

For disclosure, the Fed has publicly released extensive information on its operations, mostly on a voluntary basis. For example, it has long released a weekly summary of its balance sheet. The expanded scope of its lending activities during the financial crisis eventually led it to release a monthly report that offered more detailed information. Historically, the Fed had never released information on individual loans, such as the names of borrowers or amounts borrowed, however. In December 2010, as a result of the Dodd-Frank Act, the Fed released individual lending records for emergency facilities, revealing borrowers' identities. Going forward, individual records for discount window and open market operation transactions will be released with a two-year lag. In addition, Freedom of Information Act lawsuits filed by Bloomberg and Fox News Network resulted in the release of individual lending records for the discount window (the Fed's traditional lending facility for banks).

Although oversight and disclosure are often lumped together, they are separate issues and need not go together. Oversight relies on independent evaluation of the Fed, disclosure is an issue of what internal information the Fed releases to the public. Contrary to a common misperception, a GAO audit would not, under current law, result in the release of any confidential information identifying institutions that have borrowed from the Fed or the details of other transactions.

A potential consequence of greater oversight is that it could undermine the Fed's political independence. Most economists believe that the Fed's political independence leads to better policy outcomes and makes policy more effective by enhancing the Fed's credibility in the eyes of market participants. The challenge for Congress is to strike the right balance between a desire for the Fed to be responsive to Congress and for the Fed's decisions to be somewhat immune from political calculations. A potential drawback to greater disclosure is that publicizing the names of borrowers could potentially stigmatize them in a way that causes runs on those borrowers or causes them to shun access to needed liquidity. Either result could result in a less stable financial system. A potential benefit of publicizing borrowers is to safeguard against favoritism or other conflicts of interest.

INTRODUCTION

Congress has delegated monetary policy duties to the Federal Reserve (Fed), but retains oversight responsibilities. The Fed enjoys an unusual degree of independence from Congress and the president compared to other government agencies.[1] Proponents of these arrangements argue that this independence results in good, non-political policymaking and a high degree of credibility with financial markets.[2] Critics of the Fed argue that it performs essential government functions, yet is more opaque and unaccountable than other government agencies. Following the financial crisis, they assailed the Fed's decision to extend more than $1 trillion of assistance to the financial sector—exceeding the amount extended by the Troubled Asset Relief Program (TARP)—without any congressional input. These critics call for more oversight, transparency, and disclosure for the Fed. More specifically, critics have focused on the Government Accountability Office (GAO) audits of the Fed and the disclosure of details on the identities of borrowers and terms of loans.[3]

Some of these critics downplay the degree of Fed oversight and disclosure that already takes place, which is outlined in this report. Contrary to popular belief, GAO[4] has conducted frequent audits of the Fed since 1978, subject to statutory restrictions discussed below. In addition, the Fed's annual financial statements are audited by private sector auditors.

The Dodd-Frank Act (P.L. 111-203) resulted in an audit of the Fed's emergency activities during the financial crisis, released in July 2011, and an audit of Fed governance, released in October 2011.[5] In December 2010, as a result of the Dodd-Frank Act, the Fed released individual lending records for emergency facilities, revealing borrowers' identities for the first time. Going forward, the act requires individual records for discount window and open market operation transactions to be released with a two year lag. In addition, Freedom of Information Act lawsuits filed by *Bloomberg* and *Fox News Network* resulted in the release of individual lending records for the discount window (the Fed's traditional lending facility for banks).

Although oversight and disclosure are often lumped together, they are separate issues and need not go together. Oversight relies on independent evaluation of the Fed, disclosure is an issue of what internal information the Fed releases to the public. Contrary to a common misperception, a GAO audit would not, under current law, result in the release of any confidential information identifying institutions that have borrowed from the Fed or the details of other transactions. This report will consider the two issues separately.

The report discusses recently enacted legislation and legislation introduced in the 112th Congress. Finally, this report considers the potential impact of greater oversight and disclosure on the Fed's independence and its ability to achieve its macroeconomic and financial stability goals.

OVERSIGHT OF FEDERAL RESERVE ACTIVITIES

Before the recent financial crisis, oversight of the Fed already occurred in a number of forms. Regular congressional oversight of the Fed was, and still is, done through statutorily required semi-annual hearings with the House Financial Services Committee and the Senate Banking, Housing, and Urban Affairs Committee,[6] as well as ad hoc hearings on more focused topics, such as the Fed's response to the financial crisis.[7] Indeed, the House Financial Services Committee has a subcommittee dedicated primarily to monetary policy issues, the Subcommittee on Domestic Monetary Policy and Technology.

The term of chairman of the Federal Reserve Board of Governors lasts four years and is subject to presidential nomination and Senate confirmation. This gives the Senate a chance to review and weigh in on the Fed's performance every four years. Governors are also subject to presidential nomination and Senate confirmation, but can serve only one full term, so it is rare for the Senate to evaluate a sitting governor. Regional bank presidents and directors are not subject to Senate confirmation, but are chosen in part by the Board of Governors.

One notable difference between the Fed and most other government agencies is that there is no congressional budgetary oversight of the Fed—the Fed is self-financing and its budget is not subject to the appropriations or authorization process. Thus, there is no regular avenue for Congress to ensure that the Fed is devoting resources to congressional priorities, or to use congressional control over resources as leverage to achieve its goals.

Within the Federal Reserve system, there is an Office of Inspector General (OIG) that regularly issues reports stemming from its investigations. It also issues a semiannual report to Congress that provides an overview of its activities. The Fed's OIG "promotes integrity, economy, efficiency, and effectiveness; helps prevent and detect fraud, waste, and abuse; and strengthens the agencies' accountability to Congress and the public;"[8] it does not perform policy or economic evaluations.

Effective Congressional oversight is complicated by the complex, technical nature of monetary policymaking. There is no group with monetary policy expertise tasked by Congress with evaluating the Fed's actions. Congress could create specific oversight boards or committees that focus on the Federal Reserve. Congress could also rely on GAO audits for enhanced oversight. The congressional debate has focused on GAO audits, which are discussed in the next section.

GAO Audits

GAO is described as the "congressional watchdog," and GAO's mission is "to support the Congress in meeting its constitutional responsibilities and to help improve the performance and ensure the accountability of the federal government for the benefit of the American people."[9] Balancing Congress's need for GAO's support in fulfilling its oversight role with the congressional desire to maintain the Fed's independence has led Congress to debate the utility of GAO audits of the Fed for decades.

Contrary to popular belief, GAO has conducted numerous audits related to the Fed since 1978. GAO audits are only initiated at the request of a member or committee of Congress, and the subject of the audit is determined by the requester. Thus, the extent of attention devoted by GAO to the Fed over time depends on Congressional priorities. The Fed reported eight GAO audits related to the Fed completed in 2010, and 10 initiated but not yet complete.[10] The completion and initiation of multiple GAO audits related to the Fed in a year is not unusual –the Fed reported five audits completed and five others initiated but not yet completed in 2005.[11] Federal statute limited the scope of these audits, however.

GAO was not allowed to audit the Fed between 1933 and 1978.[12] The Federal Banking Agency Audit Act of 1978 (31 USC 714) gave GAO authority to audit the Fed's non-monetary policy functions, such as its regulatory duties and role in the payment system. It prohibited GAO from auditing Fed activities related to

1) transactions for or with a foreign central bank, government of a foreign country, or non-private international financing organization;
2) deliberations, decisions, or actions on monetary policy matters, including discount window operations, reserves of member banks, securities credit, interest on deposits, and open market operations;
3) transactions made under the direction of the Federal Open Market Committee; or
4) a part of a discussion or communication among or between members of the Board and officers and employees of the Federal Reserve System related to clauses (1)-(3) of this subsection.[13]

Although the act does not specifically mention activities taken under the Fed's emergency authority, which was widely used during the crisis, those activities were interpreted as falling under the act's restrictions. The 1978 act also included restrictions on GAO disclosure of confidential information about the financial firms subject to the Fed's policies.

These 1978 provisions are still in effect today, but significant additions in more recent acts discussed in the next section have greatly expanded the scope of GAO's audits.

Recent Legislation on Oversight

The Helping Families Save Their Homes Act (P.L. 111-22)

An amendment to the Helping Families Save Their Homes Act of 2009 (P.L. 111-22) allows GAO audits of "any action taken by the Board under ... Section 13(3) of the Federal Reserve Act with respect to a single and specific partnership or corporation." This allows GAO audits of the Maiden Lane facilities and the asset guarantees of Citigroup and Bank of America, but maintained audit restrictions on non-emergency activities and broadly-accessed emergency lending facilities, such as the Primary Dealer Credit Facility or the commercial paper facilities. In performing the audit under S. 896, GAO must maintain the confidentiality of the private documents it accesses, but cannot withhold any information requested by Members of Congress on the committees of jurisdiction.

The Dodd-Frank Act (P.L. 111-203)

Title XI of the Dodd-Frank Wall Street Reform and Consumer Protection Act of 2010 (P.L. 111- 203) allows GAO for the first time to audit open market operations, discount window lending, actions taken under emergency authority, and actions taken in response to the financial crisis for

a) the operational integrity, accounting, financial reporting, and internal controls governing the credit facility or covered transaction;
b) the effectiveness of the security and collateral policies established for the facility or covered transaction in mitigating risk to the relevant Federal reserve bank and taxpayers;
c) whether the credit facility or the conduct of a covered transaction inappropriately favors one or more specific participants over other institutions eligible to utilize the facility; and
d) the policies governing the use, selection, or payment of third-party contractors by or for any credit facility or to conduct any covered transaction.[14]

Although the legislation authorizes GAO audits on these grounds, it does not authorize GAO to conduct policy or economic evaluations of the Fed's monetary actions. In addition, GAO may not disclose confidential information in its reports or to Congress until that information is made public by the Fed, with the exception of the Fed's Maiden Lane facilities. Thus, a GAO audit would not result in the disclosure of any confidential information, such as who has borrowed from the Fed. These statutory changes were added to – as opposed to replacing – the existing statutory restrictions.

The Dodd-Frank Act mandated that GAO must audit the Fed's response to the recent crisis within a year of enactment. This audit was completed in July 2011.[15] The legislation also calls for a separate GAO audit of Federal Reserve bank governance to assess whether it produces potential or actual conflicts of interest, whether the existing system of selecting regional Federal Reserve bank directors results in directors who represent "the public without discrimination on the basis of race, creed, color, sex, or national origin, and with due but not exclusive consideration to the interests of agriculture, commerce, industry, services, labor, and consumers,"[16] the role regional banks played in the Fed's response to the crisis, and to propose reforms to regional bank governance. This audit was completed in October 2011.[17]

A brief evaluation of the July 2011 audit may provide evidence to help answer the question of whether these enhanced audit powers have increased the effectiveness of congressional oversight, and whether removing all audit restrictions in the future would be useful. Most of the information covered in the GAO audit had already been publicly released by the Fed, so there was very little that could be learned from the audit that could not have been learned elsewhere. Some of the information was summarized in a more convenient form for a lay reader, however, whereas use of the raw data would, in some cases, have required time-consuming and complex calculations to reproduce their findings. On the other hand, the presentation of some of the information was arguably sensationalized in a way that exaggerated the size and scope of the Fed's actions. For instance, GAO produced a table widely cited in the press that made it appear as if the Fed had lent $16 trillion during the crisis, although total lending from the Fed by the broadest measure never exceeded $1.6 trillion.[18] GAO generated this total by summing up all loans made by the Fed over the course of the crisis, whether their term was one day or one year. This is not a common accounting method because it makes 365 one-day loans that are rolled over each day appear 365 times larger than a one-year loan of the same amount, even though the amount extended by the Fed is the same in both cases. GAO also made some specific recommendations for the Fed to strengthen internal controls and increase disclosure.

The Dodd-Frank Act also created a Federal Reserve Vice Chairman for Supervision, and required the Vice Chairman to appear before the House Financial Services Committee and the Senate Banking, Housing, and Urban Affairs Committee semi-annually regarding the Fed's financial supervisory powers.[19]

112th Congress

In the 112th Congress, Representative Ron Paul has sponsored two bills entitled the Federal Reserve Transparency Act. Both remove all existing restrictions on GAO audits from statute, including confidentiality restrictions. H.R. 1496 calls for an audit within 12 months of enactment. H.R. 459 calls for an audit of the Fed before the end of 2012. There is a Senate companion bill to H.R. 459 sponsored by Senator Rand Paul, S. 202.

DISCLOSURE OF FEDERAL RESERVE ACTIVITIES

Until the financial crisis, statutory requirements for Fed disclosure were limited. The Fed is statutorily required to "annually make a full report of its operations" to Congress that includes a full account of open market operations.[20] This Annual Report is made publicly available.[21] The Fed is statutorily required to have its financial statements annually audited by an independent auditor.[22] This audit is published in the Fed's Annual Report. Congress also requires the Fed to produce reports on other miscellaneous topics.[23]

Despite the limited scope of statutory requirements, the Fed has publicly disclosed extensive information on its operations, and the amount of disclosure has increased over time. Indeed, much of the information about monetary policy that the Fed currently makes public is done so on a voluntarily basis. The Fed publishes data on its financial condition and transactions on a weekly basis. The Fed releases minutes from its monetary policy deliberations (Federal Open Market Committee meetings) with a three week lag, and releases transcripts of those deliberations with a five year lag. The Fed is subject to the Freedom of Information Act (FOIA), although it sometimes invokes exemptions provided in that act to deny FOIA requests.[24]

Before 2007, Fed lending to the financial system was minimal and monetary policy was limited to the buying and selling of U.S. Treasury securities. Public and Congressional interest in Fed disclosure increased in response to the significant assistance provided by the Fed to the financial sector during the financial crisis. As the crisis unfolded, the Fed has publicly released a significant amount of information on its emergency actions. The Fed has provided detailed information to the public on the general terms and eligibility of its borrowers and collateral by class for each crisis-response program.[25] It has also provided a rationale for why each crisis program has been created, and an explanation of the goals the program aims to accomplish. Beginning in June 2009, the Fed began releasing a monthly report that listed the number of and concentration among borrowers by type, the value and credit-worthiness of collateral held by type, and the interest income earned for each of its facilities.[26] Contracts with private vendors to purchase or manage assets are also posted on the New York Fed's website.

Prior to the Dodd-Frank Act, the Fed had kept confidential the identity of the borrowers from its facilities, the collateral posted in specific transactions, the terms of specific transactions, and the results of specific transactions (i.e., whether they resulted in profits or losses). As historical precedent, the Fed has had a longstanding policy of keeping confidential the identity of banks that borrow from its discount window.

Recent Legislation on Disclosure

The Emergency Economic Stabilization Act (P.L. 110-343)

For any action taken under the Fed's emergency authority (Section 13(3) of the Federal Reserve Act), the Emergency Economic Stabilization Act (P.L. 110-343) requires the Fed to report to the House Financial Services Committee and the Senate Banking, Housing, and Urban Affairs Committee on its justification for exercising Section 13(3), the terms of the assistance provided, and regular updates on the status of the assistance. It did not require the Fed to release information on the identities of borrowers or information on specific transactions.

The Dodd-Frank Act (P.L. 111-203)

For actions taken under Section 13(3) of the Federal Reserve Act, Title XI of the Dodd-Frank Act requires that the Fed provide the congressional committees of jurisdiction details on the rationale for assistance, the identity of the recipient, the date, amount, and form of assistance, collateral pledged, the material terms of the assistance, and the expected cost to the taxpayer. This information is to be provided within seven days, with updates every 30 days following. The Fed can request that this information be kept confidential and limited to the chairmen and ranking members of the committees.

The act calls for the first time for public disclosure of the identities of borrowers, amount borrowed, rate charged, and collateral pledged or assets transferred. Going forward, this information is to be disclosed within one year after a credit facility is terminated and within two years after the transaction for discount window loans or open market operations. For Fed programs created during the crisis, this information had to be publicly disclosed by December 1, 2010. The information was released on that date.[27]

Title XI also requires the Fed to create a page on its website entitled "Audit," linking to GAO reports, its financial statements, and the reports required under the Emergency Economic Stabilization Act (described above).

Title XI also requires the Fed's Inspector General to conduct a study on the impact of exemptions from the Freedom of Information Act on the ability of the public to access information on theFed's emergency facilities, discount window, and open market operations within 30 months of enactment.

Freedom of Information Act Lawsuits

The December 2010 release did not include information on discount window transactions. Separately, Bloomberg and Fox News Network sued the Federal Reserve under the Freedom of Information Act for the release of internal records pertaining to lending activities, including the discount window, for the period of August 2007 to March 2010. The Fed initially denied their requests based on the exemptions provided in the FOIA, but, as a result of the court ruling, the Fed released this information on March 31, 2011.[28]

Arguments for and against Greater Oversight and Disclosure

The Fed has argued that allowing the public to know which firms are accessing its facilities could undermine investor confidence in the institutions receiving aid because of a perception that recipients are weak or unsound. A loss of investor confidence could potentially lead to destabilizing runs on the institution's deposits, debt, or equity. If institutions feared that this would occur, the Fed argues, then the institutions would be wary of participating in the Fed's programs. A delayed release of information mitigates, but does not eliminate, these concerns. Some critics would view less Fed lending as a positive outcome, but if the premise that the Fed's lender of last resort role helps prevent financial crises by maintaining the liquidity of the financial system is accepted, then an unwillingness by institutions to access Fed facilities makes the system less safe.

Whether investors are less willing to borrow as a result of the disclosure of identities will not be apparent until the next liquidity crunch. A historical example supporting the Fed's argument would be the experience with the Reconstruction Finance Corporation (RFC) in the Great Depression. When the RFC publicized to which banks it had given loans, those banks typically experienced depositor runs.[29] A more recent example—disclosure of TARP fund recipients— provides mixed evidence. At first, TARP funds were widely disbursed, and recipients included all the major banks. At that point, there was no perceived stigma to TARP participation. Subsequently, many banks repaid TARP shares at the first opportunity, and several remaining participants have expressed concern that if they did not repay soon, investors would perceive them as weak. Arguments about investor confidence are arguably less compelling when applied to publicly disclosing collateral held by the Fed.

The granularity of information to be disclosed is a policy issue. Aggregate information about programs and activities that does not require the identification of borrowers tends to be more useful for broad policy purposes, while current information on specific transactions within the programs is of interest to investors. The Fed voluntarily released the former, but only reluctantly released the latter when compelled to by legislation and lawsuits. For oversight purposes, the former would suffice for answering most questions about taxpayer risk exposure, expected profits or losses, potential subsidies, economic effects, and evaluating the state of the financial system. The latter would be necessary for transparency around issues such as favoritism (certain firms receiving preferential treatment over similar firms).[30] Although preventing favoritism is a valid policy goal, releasing the identities of borrowers to "name and shame" them is more questionable, especially if the belief is that these programs were helpful for providing liquidity and maintaining financial stability. Naming and shaming is likely to result in less uptake of the programs in the future. If the belief is that these lending programs are not helpful, eliminating the programs would appear to be a rational option, rather than undermining their effectiveness by stigmatizing recipients.

Greater disclosure and outside evaluation could potentially help Congress perform its oversight duties more effectively. An argument against increasing Fed oversight would be that it could be perceived as reducing the Fed's operational independence. Chairman Bernanke has argued that "The general repeal of (the audit) exemption would serve only to increase the perceived influence of Congress on monetary policy decisions, which would undermine the confidence the public and the markets have in the Fed."[31] Most economists believe that the Fed's independence to carry out day-to-day decisions about monetary policy, unburdened by short-term political considerations, strengthens the Fed's credibility in the eyes of the private sector that it will achieve its mandated goal of price stability. Greater credibility is perceived to strengthen the effectiveness of monetary policy on the economy. This independence is seen as consistent with the democratic process because the Fed's mandate to pursue price and economic stability has been given to it by Congress, and use of policy instruments to achieve these goals is viewed as relatively technocratic in nature.[32]

The Fed's unprecedented response to the financial crisis moved it into new policy areas involving decisions that were arguably more political in nature, such as deciding which financial actors should be eligible to access Fed credit. New policy instruments were also potentially riskier than the discount window, and, unlike the discount window, were not explicitly endorsed by legislation at the time (many were authorized under its broad emergency authority). At this point, the emergency programs are winding down, lending is low, and Fed activities have shifted back to the traditional buying and selling of U.S. Treasury securities. As a result, some rationales raised during the crisis for greater oversight and disclosure are waning. Were another crisis to occur, Fed lending could potentially scale up quickly again, however.

Although few policymakers argue for total independence or total disclosure and oversight, the policy challenge is to strike the right balance between Fed independence and Fed accountability. In February 2010 testimony, Chairman Bernanke advocated striking such a balance:

> we understand that the unusual nature of (the emergency credit and liquidity) facilities creates a special obligation to assure the Congress and the public of the integrity of their operation. Accordingly, we would welcome a review by the GAO of the Federal Reserve's management of all facilities created under emergency authorities. In particular, we would

> support legislation authorizing the GAO to audit the operational integrity, collateral policies, use of third-party contractors, accounting, financial reporting, and internal controls of these special credit and liquidity facilities.... We are also prepared to support legislation that would require the release of the identities of the firms that participated in each special facility after an appropriate delay. It is important that the release occur after a lag that is sufficiently long that investors will not view an institution's use of one of the facilities as a possible indication of ongoing financial problems, thereby undermining market confidence in the institution or discouraging use of any future facility that might become necessary to protect the U.S. economy.33

Of course, Congress may ultimately settle on a different balance between the two than Chairman Bernanke has prescribed.

End Notes

[1] For more information, see CRS Report RL31056, *Economics of Federal Reserve Independence*, by Marc Labonte.

[2] See, for example, Frederic Mishkin, "Politicians Are Threatening the Fed's Independence," Wall Street Journal, September 29, 2011, http://online.wsj.com/article/SB10001424052970 20483130457659 7200646525870.html. Economist William Poole makes the case that the Fed's independence is valuable, but that its role in the crisis has undermined its independence. See William Poole, "The Bernanke Question," July 28, 2009, http:// www.cato.org/ pub_display.php?pub_id=10388. For a review of the economic literature on whether independence promotes better policy, see CRS Report RL31955, *Central Bank Independence and Economic Performance: What Does the Evidence Show?*, by Marc Labonte and Gail E. Makinen.

[3] See, for example, Mark Calabria, Testimony before U.S. House of Representatives, Committee on Financial Services, October 4, 2011, http://financialservices.house.gov/UploadedFiles /100411calabria.pdf.

[4] GAO was formerly known as the General Accounting Office.

[5] For details of the Fed's actions during the financial crisis, see CRS Report RL34427, *Financial Turmoil: Federal Reserve Policy Responses*, by Marc Labonte.

[6] Section 2B of the Federal Reserve Act (12 USC 225b). These hearings and reporting requirements were established by the Full Employment Act of 1978 (P.L. 95-523, 92 Stat 1897), also known as the Humphrey-Hawkins Act, and renewed in the American Homeownership and Economic Opportunity Act of 2000 (P.L. 106-569). Since 2000, the Chairman has not been required to testify before both committees semi-annually, but has continued to do so.

[7] In response to the financial crisis, Congress also created a special legislative branch committee, the Congressional Oversight Panel (COP), and an executive branch inspector general, the Special Inspector General for the Troubled Asset Relief Program (SIGTARP) tasked with

providing oversight of TARP for Congress. While both were focused on TARP, both occasionally analyzed the Fed's emergency operations, particularly those that overlapped with TARP. COP ceased operations in 2011.

[8] Federal Reserve, Office Of Inspector General's Mission Statement, July 19, 2011, http://www .federalreserve.gov/oig/ mission.htm.

[9] http://www.gao.gov/about/index.html.

[10] Federal Reserve, *97th Annual Report 2010*, June 2011, p. 407, http://www.federalreserve.gov /publications/annualreport/files/2010-annual-report.pdf.

[11] Federal Reserve, *92nd Annual Report 2005*, June 2006, p. 326, http://www.federalreserve. gov/ boarddocs/rptcongress/ annual05/pdf/ar05.pdf.

[12] General Accounting Office, "Federal Reserve System Audits," Testimony by Charles Bowsher before the House Committee on Banking, Finance, and Urban Affairs, GAO-GGD-94-44, October 27, 1993. Before 1978, GAO could only audit the Fed in its role as fiscal agent of the U.S. Treasury.

[13] 31 USC 714 (b).

[14] P.L. 111-203 § (b)(2).

[15] U.S. Government Accountability Office, *Federal Reserve System: Opportunities Exist to Strengthen Policies and Processes for Managing Emergency Assistance*, GAO-11-696, Jul 21, 2011, http://www.gao.gov/new.items/ d11696.pdf.

[16] P.L. 111-203, § 1109(b) quoting 12 USC. § 302.

[17] U.S. Government Accountability Office, *Federal Reserve Bank Governance: Opportunities Exist to Broaden Director Recruitment Efforts and Increase Transparency*, GAO-12-18, October 19, 2011, http://www.gao.gov/ new.items/d1218.pdf.

[18] U.S. Government Accountability Office, *Federal Reserve System: Opportunities Exist to Strengthen Policies and Processes for Managing Emergency Assistance*, GAO-11-696, July 21, 2011, Table 8, p. 131, http://www.gao.gov/ new.items/d11696.pdf.

[19] Section 10(12) of the Federal Reserve Act (12 USC 247b). Before the Dodd-Frank Act, there was only one vice chairman of the Board of Governors with general responsibilities.

[20] Section 10(7) and Section 10(10) of the Federal Reserve Act (12 USC 247 and 12 USC 247a, respectively).

[21] Annual reports can be accessed at http://www.federalreserve.gov/publications/annual-report /default.htm.

[22] Section 11B of the Federal Reserve Act (12 USC 248b).

[23] Other Fed reports to Congress can be accessed at http://www.federalreserve.gov/publications /other-reports/ default.htm.

[24] The nine FOIA exemptions and their relevance to the Fed are detailed at http://www. Federal reserve.gov/generalinfo/ foia/exemptions.cfm.

[25] All of the information outlined in this paragraph can be accessed at the Fed's website at http://www.federalreserve.gov/monetarypolicy/bst.htm.

[26] Federal Reserve Board of Governors, *Federal Reserve System Monthly Report on Credit and Liquidity Programs and the Balance Sheet*.

[27] It can be accessed at http://www.federalreserve.gov/newsevents/reform_transaction.htm.

[28] Bloomberg LP v. Board of Governors of the Federal Reserve System, U.S. District Court, Southern District of New York (Manhattan), No. 08-9595.

[29] James Butkiewicz, "The Reconstruction Finance Corporation, the Gold Standard, and the Banking Panic of 1933," *Southern Economic Journal*, vol. 66, no. 2, October 1999, p. 271.

[30] Another option for addressing these types of questions would be to allow GAO, the Fed's Inspector General, or some other outside group to investigate confidential material without releasing it to the public.

[31] Chairman Ben Bernanke, "Don't Strip the Fed of Supervisory Power," *Valley News*, December 1, 2009, p. A6. See also Federal Reserve Vice Chairman Donald Kohn, "Federal Reserve Independence," Testimony before the Subcommittee on Domestic Monetary Policy and Technology, House Financial Services Committee, July 9, 2009.

[32] See CRS Report RL31056, *Economics of Federal Reserve Independence*, by Marc Labonte.

[33] Chairman Ben S. Bernanke, Semiannual Monetary Policy Report to the Congress, Before the Committee on Financial Services, U.S. House of Representatives, Washington, DC, February 24, 2010.

In: The Federal Reserve ISBN: 978-1-62081-034-7
Editors: G. R. Conley and A. A. Sanford© 2012 Nova Science Publishers, Inc.

Chapter 2

FEDERAL RESERVE BANK GOVERNANCE: OPPORTUNITIES EXIST TO BROADEN DIRECTOR RECRUITMENT EFFORTS AND INCREASE TRANSPARENCY*

United States Government Accountability Office

WHY GAO DID THIS STUDY

Events surrounding the 2007 financial crisis raised questions about the governance of the 12 Federal Reserve Banks (Reserve Banks), particularly the boards of directors' roles in activities related to supervision and regulation. The Dodd-Frank Wall Street Reform and Consumer Protection Act required GAO to review the governance of the Reserve Banks. This report (1) analyzes the level of diversity on the boards of directors and assesses the extent to which the process of identifying possible directors and appointing them results in diversity on the boards, (2) evaluates the effectiveness of policies and practices for identifying and managing conflicts of interest for Reserve Bank directors, and (3) compares Reserve Bank governance practices with the practices of selected organizations. To conduct this work, GAO reviewed bylaws, policies, and board minutes for each Reserve Bank, conducted a

* This is an edited, reformatted and augmented version of Highlights of GAO-12-18, a report to congressional requesters, dated October 2011.

survey of directors who served in 2010, reviewed governance policies at comparable institutions, and interviewed officials from the Board of Governors of the Federal Reserve System (Federal Reserve Board) and Reserve Banks, directors from each bank, and selected academics.

WHAT GAO RECOMMENDS

GAO makes four recommendations to the Federal Reserve Board aimed at enhancing the diversity of the Reserve Bank boards, strengthening policies for managing conflicts of interest, and enhancing transparency related to board governance. The Federal Reserve Board agreed with GAO's recommendations and said that it believes all have merit and will work to implement them. The Reserve Banks also said that they will give serious consideration to implementing the recommendations.

WHAT GAO FOUND

The Federal Reserve Act requires each Reserve Bank to be governed by a nine-member board—three Class A directors elected by member banks to represent their interests, three Class B directors elected by member banks to represent the public, and three Class C directors that are appointed by the Federal Reserve Board to represent the public. The diversity of Reserve Bank boards was limited from 2006 to 2010. For example, in 2006 minorities accounted for 13 of 108 director positions, and in 2010 they accounted for 15 of 108 director positions. Specifically, in 2010 Reserve Bank directors included 78 white men, 15 white women, 12 minority men, and 3 minority women. According to the Federal Reserve Act, Class B and C directors are to be elected with due but not exclusive consideration to the interests of agriculture, commerce, industry, services, labor, and consumer representation. During this period, labor and consumer groups had less representation than other industries. In 2010, 56 of the 91 directors that responded to GAO's survey had financial markets experience. Reserve Banks generally review the current demographics of their boards and use a combination of personal networking and community outreach efforts to identify potential candidates for directors. Reserve Bank officials said that they generally limit their director search efforts to senior executives. GAO's analysis of Equal Employment

Opportunity Commission data found that diversity among senior executives is generally limited. While some Reserve Banks recruit more broadly, GAO recommends that the Federal Reserve Board encourage all Reserve Banks to consider ways to help enhance the economic and demographic diversity of perspectives on the boards, including by broadening their potential candidate pool.

The Federal Reserve System mitigates and manages the actual and potential conflicts of interest by, among other things, defining the directors' roles and responsibilities, monitoring adherence to conflict-of-interest policies, and establishing internal controls to identify and manage potential conflicts. Reserve Bank directors are often affiliated with a variety of financial firms, nonprofits, and private and public companies. As the financial services industry evolves, more companies are becoming involved in financial services or interconnected with financial institutions. As a result, directors of all three classes can have ties to the financial sector. While these relationships may not give rise to actual conflicts of interest, they can create the appearance of a conflict as illustrated by the participation of director-affiliated institutions in the Federal Reserve System's emergency programs. Moreover, some critics question the Reserve Bank boards' involvement in supervision and regulation activities. GAO found that directors have a limited role in these activities, including voting on certain budget and personnel actions. Moreover, some Reserve Banks have further restricted the responsibilities of Class A directors, prohibiting their involvement in any personnel or budget decisions for this function. However, most Reserve Banks' bylaws do not document the role of the board in supervision and regulation. To increase transparency, GAO recommends that all Reserve Banks clearly document the directors' role in supervision and regulation activities in their bylaws. One option for addressing directors' conflicts of interest is for the Reserve Bank to request a waiver from the Federal Reserve Board, which, according to officials, is rare. Most Reserve Banks do not have a process for formally requesting such waivers. To strengthen governance practices and increase transparency, GAO recommends that the Reserve Banks develop and document a process for requesting conflict waivers for directors. Further, GAO recommends that the Reserve Banks publicly disclose when a waiver is granted, as appropriate.

The Federal Reserve System's governance practices are generally similar to those of selected central banks and comparable institutions such as bank holding companies and have similar selection procedures for directors. Further, most have similar accountability measures such as annual performance reviews. However, Reserve Bank governance practices tend to be less transparent than those of these institutions. For instance, comparable organizations make information on their board committees and ethics policies available on their websites; most Reserve banks do not. To further enhance transparency of Reserve Bank governance, GAO recommends that Reserve Banks make public key governance documents, such as bylaws, ethics policies, and committee assignments, by posting them to their websites.

Abbreviations

ABCP	asset-backed commercial paper
ABS	asset-backed security
AIG	American International Group, Inc.
AIGFP	AIG Financial Products Corp.
AMLF	Asset-Backed Commercial Paper Money Market Mutual Fund Liquidity Facility
CDO	collateralized debt obligation
CEO	chief executive officer
CFPB	Bureau of Consumer Financial Protection
CPFF	Commercial Paper Funding Facility
DMLF	Direct Money Market Mutual Fund Lending Facility
ECB	European Central Bank
EEO-1	Employer Information Report
EEOC	Equal Employment Opportunity Commission
FINRA	Financial Industry Regulation Authority
FOMC	Federal Open Market Committee
FRAM	Federal Reserve Administrative Manual
FRBNY	Federal Reserve Bank of New York
FRBR	Federal Reserve Bank of Richmond
FSOC	Financial Stability Oversight Council
JPMC	JP Morgan Chase & Co.
MBS	mortgage-backed security
MMMF	money market mutual funds
MMIFF	Money Market Investor Funding Facility
NAICS	North American Industrial Classification System
OECD	Organisation for Economic Co-operation and Development
RBA	Reserve Bank of Australia
RBOPS	Division of Reserve Bank Operations and Payment Systems

RCF	revolving credit facility
RMBS	residential mortgage-backed security
SEC	Securities and Exchange Commission
SPF	securities borrowing facility
SPV	special-purpose vehicle
TAF	Term Action Facility
TALF	Term Asset-Backed Securities Loan Facility

October 19, 2011

Congressional Addressees

The Federal Reserve System, which consists of the Board of Governors of the Federal Reserve System (Federal Reserve Board), 12 regional Reserve Banks, and the Federal Open Market Committee (FOMC), played a key role in the U.S. government's policy responses to the financial crisis that began in the summer of 2007.[1] From late 2007 through mid-2010, Reserve Banks provided more than a trillion dollars in emergency loans to the financial sector to address strains in credit markets and to avert failures of individual institutions believed to be a threat to the stability of the financial system. The scale and nature of this assistance amounted to a rare and significant exercise of the Federal Reserve System's emergency powers as a lender of last resort.

Unlike the Federal Reserve Board, the Reserve Banks are not federal agencies. Each Reserve Bank is a federally chartered corporation with a board of directors. The membership of each Reserve Bank board includes three directors who represent commercial banks that are members of the Federal Reserve System and six directors who represent the public. During the crisis, the Federal Reserve System came under scrutiny when it became known that several institutions that borrowed from the emergency programs were affiliated with Reserve Bank directors. Some Members of Congress and others raised concerns about actual or potential conflicts of interest that may have been created by these affiliations and the possibility that some directors had exerted influence on the emergency lending activities of the Reserve Banks. More broadly, the Reserve Bank board structure that includes three directors who represent banks supervised by the Reserve Banks caused public concern about the governance of the banks, including the selection and roles of directors and the extent to which directors elected to represent the public do so. For example, questions were raised as to whether the directors representing member banks had any involvement in the Reserve Banks' role in supervising member banks.

Title XI of the Dodd-Frank Wall Street Reform and Consumer Protection Act (Dodd-Frank Act) contains provisions intended to enhance transparency and accountability related to the Federal Reserve System's emergency lending activities as well as a change to the elections of Reserve Bank presidents. As part of this title, the Dodd-Frank Act directed us to review various issues related to the governance of the Federal Reserve Banks.[2] Accordingly, the objectives of this report are to (1) analyze the level of diversity on the boards of directors and assess the extent to which the process of identifying possible directors and appointing them results in diversity on the boards of directors, (2) evaluate the effectiveness of policies and practices for identifying and managing conflicts of interest for Reserve bank directors, and (3) compare Federal Reserve bank governance practices with the practices of selected organizations.[3] Appendix I reports on the Reserve Banks' involvement in the establishment and implementation of the emergency programs.

SCOPE AND METHODOLOGY

To determine the extent to which the current system of appointing Reserve Bank directors effectively ensures that they are elected without discrimination on the basis of race, creed, color, sex, or national origin, and that, for some directors, they are elected with due but not exclusive consideration to the interests of agriculture, commerce, industry, services, labor, and consumers, as required by section 4 of the Federal Reserve Act, we reviewed the Reserve Banks' processes for identification, nomination, and selection of directors. We created a descriptive profile of the demographic characteristics, including race, gender, and industry, of Reserve Bank directors from 2006 through 2010. We used (1) the demographic characteristics of directors obtained from the Federal Reserve Board, and (2) the demographic characteristics of executives who would likely meet the criteria for potential directors using Equal Employment Opportunity Commission (EEOC) data.[4] We determined whether the diversity trends of Reserve Bank directors are generally consistent with the trends illustrated by the Employer Information Report (EEO-1) data.[5] The EEO-1 data represent the pool of potential candidates with the requisite skills and experience from which the Federal Reserve generally selects directors. To assess the reliability of the Federal Reserve Board data, we interviewed Federal Reserve Board staff about steps they took to maintain the integrity and reliability of the database. To assess the reliability of the EEO-1 data, we reviewed documentation related to the data and interviewed EEOC officials on the methods used to collect data and checks performed to ensure data reliability. We believe that these data are sufficiently reliable for the purpose of our analysis. Also, to obtain baseline information from all current directors on a cross section of high-level issues, we conducted a web-based survey of the 105 Reserve Bank directors that served for the full year during 2010. Of the 105 directors surveyed, 91 responded to the survey overall. However, the number of responses to individual questions varied. We collected and summarized additional information from these directors, such as their other board positions, prior employment, and education. For a full description of the methodology of the survey, see appendix II. To assess the extent to which Federal Reserve Banks' processes for identification, nomination, and selection of directors result in diversity, we reviewed documentation on the process and interviewed officials from Federal Reserve Board and Reserve Banks.

To examine whether there are actual or potential conflicts of interests created when certain directors of Reserve Banks are elected by member banks, we reviewed and summarized the selection procedures for Reserve Bank directors, and their roles and responsibilities identified in current Federal Reserve System documents and those included in the Federal Reserve Act. We surveyed all Reserve Bank directors who served for the full year during 2010 to collect their perception of their roles and responsibilities and to determine whether they are aware of any past or present conflict of interest. Also, we interviewed selected Reserve Bank directors and Reserve Bank officials from each Reserve Bank to collect information on directors' roles and responsibilities, any conflict of interest concerns and procedures for addressing the appearance of or actual conflicts, and potential changes to Reserve Bank governance. Specifically, at each of the 12 Reserve Banks, we interviewed at least one director from each class (A, B, and C), all board and audit committee chairs, the president, general counsel or ethics officer, and corporate secretary. In addition, to identify any discussions on instances of potential or actual conflicts of interest during board meetings, we reviewed board minutes for each of the 12 Reserve Banks for the period of November 2007 to October 2010. To address the Reserve Bank directors' involvement in the establishment and operations of the Federal Reserve emergency programs, we leveraged our work from the recent Federal Reserve Emergency Program review, which conducted related work under the Dodd-Frank Act.[6] We reviewed relevant documents from each of the 12 Reserve Banks, including bylaws, procurement policies and any policies for waivers to the Federal Reserve Board's policies on director eligibility, qualifications, and rotation.

We also reviewed Reserve Bank board minutes to help determine the extent of the directors' involvement in any activities associated with the emergency programs and supervision and regulation matters. In addition, we interviewed a sample of directors and relevant Reserve Bank officials as noted earlier to determine the directors' involvement in the implementation and operation of the programs.

To compare Reserve Bank governance practices with the practices of selected organizations, we reviewed literature on current best practices for governance within major financial institutions, analyzed similar institutions in other countries or the United States to evaluate best practices or alternative structures, and relied on the results of our work done for our other objectives. We examined how the Federal Reserve System's governance practices compare with relevant practices at selected foreign central banks, a self-regulatory organization, a government-sponsored enterprise, and several large bank holding companies. For the foreign central banks, we contacted officials at foreign central banks in Australia, Canada, the European Union, and the United Kingdom to obtain governance documents and we analyzed governance policies and practices in order to compare governance of the Reserve Banks with governance of other foreign central banks. We spoke to academic researchers knowledgeable about central bank governance. We verified the accuracy of our analysis and interpretations of governance documents by requesting comments on the relevant draft sections from each of the central banks included in our review. We incorporated their comments as appropriate. For the self-regulatory organization and the government-sponsored entity, we identified and analyzed the relevant governance policies and practices of the Financial Industry Regulation Authority (FINRA) and for the cooperative system, the Federal Home Loan Banks (FHLBanks). To verify the accuracy of our analysis, we spoke with officials from these entities and obtained comments on the relevant sections of a draft of this report. Finally, for private corporations, we interviewed an industry group and some academic researchers knowledgeable about corporate governance and analyzed the governance practices of the 10 largest bank holding companies and compared them with the governance policies and practices of the previously discussed organizations.

We conducted this performance audit from July 2010 to July 2011 in accordance with generally accepted government auditing standards. Those standards require that we plan and perform the audit to obtain sufficient, appropriate evidence to provide a reasonable basis for our findings and conclusions based on our audit objectives. We believe that the evidence obtained provides a reasonable basis for our findings and conclusions based on our audit objectives.

BACKGROUND

Overview of the Federal Reserve System

The Federal Reserve Act of 1913 established the Federal Reserve System as the country's central bank.[7] The Federal Reserve Act made the Federal Reserve System an independent, decentralized bank to better ensure that monetary policy would be based on a broad economic perspective from all regions of the country. The Federal Reserve Board has defined the term "monetary policy" as the actions undertaken by a central bank, such as the Federal Reserve System, to influence the availability and cost of money and credit to help promote national economic goals. The Federal Reserve Act of 1913, as amended, gave the Federal Reserve System responsibility for setting monetary policy. The Federal Reserve System consists of three parts: the Federal Reserve Board, Reserve Banks, and the FOMC.

The Federal Reserve Board is a federal agency located in Washington, D.C., that is responsible for maintaining the stability of financial markets; supervising financial, bank, and thrift holding companies, state-chartered banks that are members of the Federal Reserve System, and the U.S. operations of foreign banking organizations; establishing monetary policy; and providing general supervision over the operations of the Reserve Banks.[8] The top officials of the Federal Reserve Board are the seven members of the Board of Governors who are appointed by the president and confirmed by the U.S. Senate. Although the Federal Reserve Board is required to report to Congress on its activities, its decisions do not have to be approved by either the President or Congress.

The Federal Reserve System is divided into 12 districts. Each district is served by a regional Reserve Bank. Most Reserve Banks have one or more branches, adding to a total of 24 branches (see figure 1). Unlike the Federal Reserve Board, the Reserve Banks are not federal agencies. Each Reserve Bank is a federally chartered corporation with a board of directors and member banks who are stockholders in the Reserve Banks. The membership of each Reserve Bank board of directors is determined by a process established by statute that is intended to ensure that each bank board represents both the public and member banks in its district. Under the Federal Reserve Act,

Reserve Banks are subject to the general supervision of the Federal Reserve Board. The Federal Reserve Board has delegated some of its supervisory responsibilities to the Reserve Banks, such as responsibility for examining bank and thrift holding companies and state member banks under rules, regulations and policies established by the Federal Reserve Board. The Federal Reserve Act authorizes the Reserve Banks to make discount window loans, in accordance with the rules and regulations prescribed by the Federal Reserve Board, and to execute monetary policy operations at the direction of the FOMC.[9] The Reserve Banks also provide payment services, such as check clearing and wire transfers, to depository institutions, the Treasury, and government agencies. The provision of these payment services to depository institutions is subject to the full cost recovery provisions of the Monetary Control Act of 1980. Reserve Banks also provide cash services to financial institutions and serve as the Treasury's Fiscal Agent.

The FOMC plays a central role in the execution of the Federal Reserve System's monetary policy mandate to promote price stability and maximum employment. The FOMC consists of the seven members of the Board of Governors, the president of the Federal Reserve Bank of New York, and four other Reserve Bank presidents who serve on a rotating basis. All presidents participate in FOMC deliberations even though not all vote. The FOMC is responsible for directing open market operations to influence the total amount of money and credit available in the economy. The Federal Reserve Bank of New York (FRBNY) carries out FOMC directives on open market operations by engaging in purchases or sales of certain securities, typically U.S. government securities, in the secondary market.

The Federal Reserve Board and the Reserve Banks are subject to an annual independent audit of their financial statements by a public accounting firm.[10] In addition, each Reserve Bank has an internal auditor who is responsible to the Reserve Bank's board of directors. The Federal Reserve Board's Division of Reserve Bank Operations and Payment Systems (RBOPS) performs periodic examinations on 4 of 12 Reserve Banks each year on a range of oversight activities and assesses compliance with Federal Reserve Board policies. The Federal Reserve Board's Office of Inspector General also conducts audits, reviews, and investigations related to the Federal Reserve Board's programs and operations, including those programs and operations that have been delegated to the Reserve Banks by the Federal Reserve Board. Finally, we may conduct a number of reviews each year to look at specific aspects of the Federal Reserve System's activities.

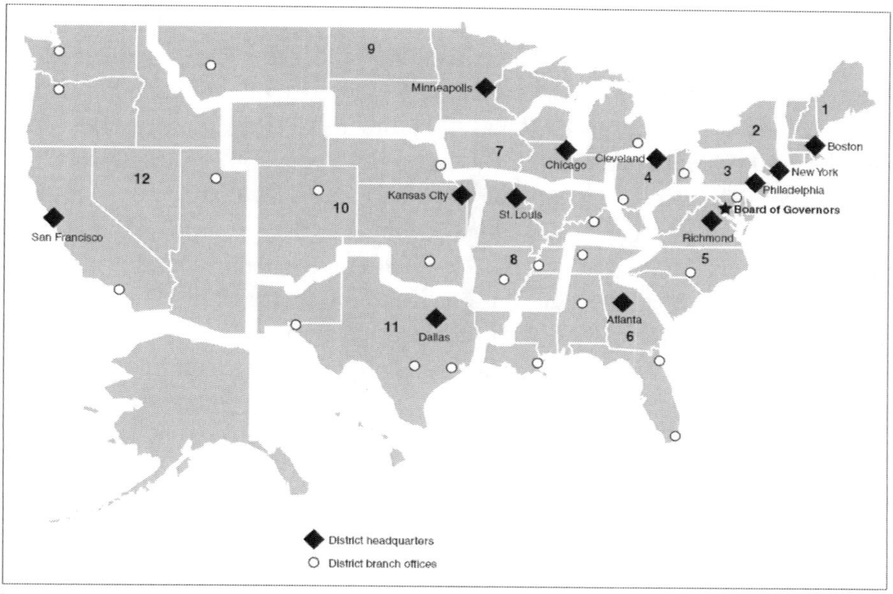

Sources: Federal Reserve Board (data); MapInfo (map).

Figure 1. Federal Reserve Districts, Reserve Banks, and Their Branch Locations.

All national banks—U.S. commercial banks that are chartered by the federal government through the Office of the Comptroller of the Currency—are required to be members of the Federal Reserve System. Banks chartered by the states may elect to become members of the Federal Reserve System if they meet certain requirements set by the Federal Reserve Board. Member banks must subscribe to stock in their Reserve Bank in an amount that is related to the size of the member bank. Holding of the stock does not confer any rights of ownership and the member bank may not sell or trade the Federal Reserve district bank stock. Member banks receive a statutory fixed annual dividend of 6 percent on their stock and may vote for six of the nine members of the board of directors of the Reserve Bank.

Reserve Bank and Branch Structure

Governance can be broadly described as the process of providing leadership, direction, and accountability in fulfilling an organization's mission, meeting objectives, and providing stewardship of an organization's resources.

Because the Reserve Bank boards are supervised by the Federal Reserve Board and their authority is constrained by both provisions of the Federal Reserve Act and guidelines of the Federal Reserve Board, among other things, they are not typical corporate boards of directors. However, Reserve Bank boards are the focal points of the Reserve Banks' governance framework that also includes the broad oversight of the Federal Reserve Board.

The Federal Reserve Act established nine-member boards of directors to govern each of the 12 Reserve Banks. Each board is split equally into three classes. Class A directors represent the member banks, while Class B and C directors represent the public with, as required by the Federal Reserve Act, "due but not exclusive consideration to the interests of agriculture, commerce, industry, services, labor, and consumers." As required by the Federal Reserve Act, six of the nine directors, Class A and Class B, are elected by the member banks, and the remaining three, the Class C directors, are appointed by the Federal Reserve Board. Figure 2 illustrates how the directors of the Reserve Banks are chosen and their roles in appointing Reserve Bank presidents.[11]

The process for selecting the boards of directors of the Reserve Banks is outlined in the Federal Reserve Act. The Federal Reserve Act requires that the member banks of each Reserve Bank District be classified into three groups consisting of banks of similar capitalization—small, medium, and large.[12] Each group is responsible for one of the three Class A directorships and one of the three Class B directorships. Each member bank in the group may nominate a candidate for an open directorship within its group. Once nominations close, each member bank in the group receives the list of nominees and a ballot to vote in the election. Directors serve 3-year terms, and the terms are staggered so that one position in each class becomes vacant every year. Although directors can be reelected to an indefinite number of terms, the Federal Reserve Board recommends that the Reserve Banks follow a limit of two consecutive appointments for a given director.

The Federal Reserve Act does not prescribe how the Federal Reserve Board is to identify and appoint the candidates for Class C directors. Pursuant to the Federal Reserve Act, one Class C director, who must be a person of "tested banking experience," is designated by the Federal Reserve Board as chairman of the Reserve Bank board of directors, and the Federal Reserve Board also designates another Class C director as deputy chairman. The Federal Reserve Act provides that the chairman of the board, like all Class C directors, cannot be an officer, director, employee, or stockholder of any bank. The Federal Reserve Board policy extends this limitation to prevent affiliations by Class B and Class C directors with any thrift, credit union, bank holding company, foreign bank, and other similar institutions and affiliates. Additionally, the Federal Reserve Act states that Class C directors must have been residents of the district of their Reserve Bank for 2 years prior to appointment. As with the election of Class A and B directors, the appointment of Class C directors is staggered so that one director position becomes vacant every year. The Federal Reserve Board has established a policy of appointing a given Class C director to no more than two terms. See table 1 for a detailed description of the requirements for selection of all three classes of directors.

Nine of the 12 Reserve Banks also have branch offices, which provide banking services, and in some cases house supervision employees. The branches are subject to the governance of the Reserve Banks and their boards of directors, as well as to oversight from the Federal Reserve Board. Twenty-three of the 24 branches have boards of seven directors, four of which are appointed by the Reserve Bank and three of which are appointed by the Federal Reserve Board. One branch (Helena) comprised five directors, three of which are appointed by the Reserve Bank, and two of which are appointed by the Federal Reserve Board. The chair of the branch office board is selected from the members appointed by the Federal Reserve Board. This report focuses primarily on the governance practices at the Reserve Banks and not branch offices.

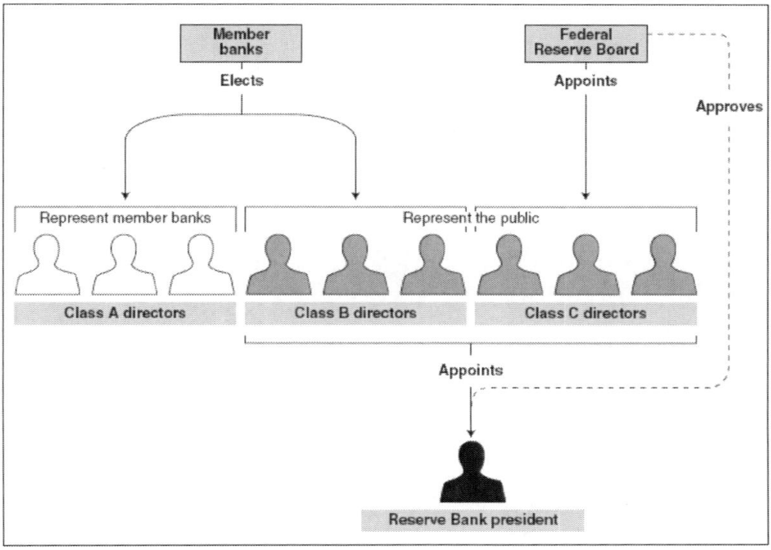

Source: GAO presentation of Federal Reserve Board information.

Figure 2. Election and Appointment of Reserve Bank President and Directors.

Table 1. Requirements for Selection of Directors, after the Enactment of the Dodd-Frank Act

Director class	Description of the requirements for selection
A	• Elected by member banks • Elected, without discrimination on the basis of race, creed, color, sex or national origin, to represent the stockholding banks • May be an officer, director, or employee of a member bank
B	• Elected by member banks • Elected, without discrimination on the basis of race, creed, color, sex, or national origin, to represent the public • Chosen with due but not exclusive consideration to the interests of agriculture, commerce, industry, services, labor, and consumers • Cannot be officers, directors, or employees of any bank
C	• Appointed by the Federal Reserve Board • Chosen, without discrimination on the basis of race, creed, color, sex, or national origin, to represent the public • Chosen with due but not exclusive consideration to the interests of agriculture, commerce, industry, services, labor and consumers • Cannot be officers, directors, employees, or stockholders of any bank or bank, financial, or thrift holding company, although the chair must be a person of "tested banking experience[a] • Must have been residents of the district of their Reserve Bank for 2 years prior to appointment

Source: GAO summary of Federal Reserve System information.

Notes: Section 4(13) of the Federal Reserve Act provides that no Members of Congress shall be directors of Reserve Bank boards.

[a] The chairs and deputy chairs of the Reserve Bank boards are appointed from this class by the Federal Reserve Board.

Roles and Responsibilities of Reserve Bank Directors

The three principal functions of Reserve Bank directors are to (1) participate in the formulation of national monetary and credit policies; (2) oversee the general management of the Reserve Bank, including its branches; and (3) act as a link between the Federal Reserve Bank and the community.

The Reserve Bank boards have the ability to influence the nation's monetary policy in three primary ways (1) by providing input on economic conditions to the Reserve Bank president, which is used by some presidents in their reports to the FOMC about regional economic conditions; (2) by participating in the establishment every 2 weeks of a discount rate recommendation sent to the Federal Reserve Board for its consideration; and (3) for the Class B and C directors, by appointing the Reserve Bank president and first vice president.

- **Beige Books:** The Reserve Banks publish a *Summary of Commentary on Current Economic Conditions*, informally known as the Beige Book, eight times per year. The Beige Book is a compilation of reports on current district economic conditions filed by each Reserve Bank drawing on its network of district contacts. Reserve Banks' directors' observations on the economy may be included in the Reserve Bank's Beige Book report. The Reserve Banks take turns summarizing economic information for the Beige Book and writing the report's summary. The FOMC and the Federal Reserve Board use the Beige Books—which are published 2 weeks before each FOMC meeting—to inform their decisions on discount rates and the Federal Funds Rate target.[13]
- **Discount rate:** The Federal Reserve Act authorizes each Reserve Bank to establish, subject to review and determination by the Federal Reserve Board, discount rates.[14] The statute provides that each Reserve Bank shall establish such rates every 14 days or more often if deemed necessary by the Federal Reserve Board. Reserve Bank directors typically conduct a conference call every 14 days, unless they are holding an in-person meeting, to vote on the discount rate. The rate established by the Reserve Bank must be approved by the Federal Reserve Board.
- **Reserve Bank president:** Each Reserve Bank board's Class B and Class C directors appoint, with the approval of the Federal Reserve Board, the president of their Reserve Bank. The president of the Reserve Bank uses the information (s)he gathers from the Reserve Bank's board of directors, research department, and a variety of other sources to influence monetary policy through (her)his position on the FOMC. The FOMC sets the Federal Funds Rate target and monitors and directs the Open Market Operations necessary to achieve that rate. All of the 12 Reserve Bank presidents attend and participate in deliberations at each meeting of the FOMC. As noted earlier, the president of FRBNY has a permanent voting position and the other 11 presidents rotate, on an annual basis, among four voting positions on the FOMC. Figure 3 illustrates how the members of the FOMC are selected.

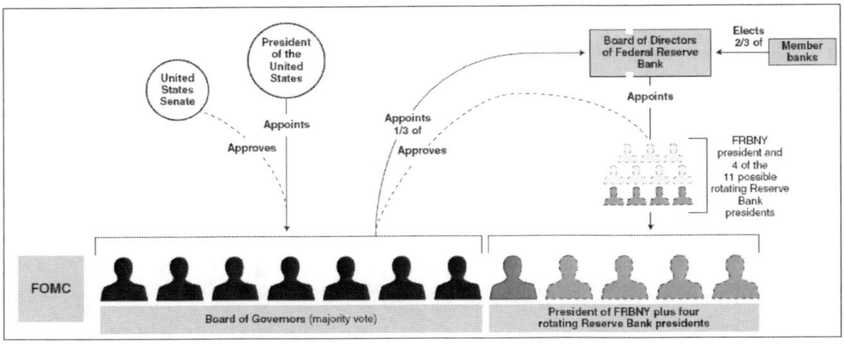

Source: GAO presentation of Federal Reserve Board information.

Figure 3. Selection of Federal Open Market Committee Members.

Pursuant to the Federal Reserve Act, the operations of each Reserve Bank are to be conducted under the supervision and control of its board of directors. The Reserve Bank directors have similar operational roles and responsibilities of directors of most private corporations, subject to some limitations imposed by the Federal Reserve Act or the Federal Reserve System. Reserve Bank boards of directors are authorized to appoint officers and to define their duties, and to prescribe bylaws under which the Reserve Banks' general business may be conducted. [15] The Federal Reserve Act charges each board of directors with administering the affairs of the Reserve Bank "fairly and impartially and without discrimination in favor of or against any member bank or banks." The directors approve the bank and bank branches' budgets and evaluate the performance of key leadership.[16] Except for Class A directors, the directors also choose the president and first vice president.[17] The board s of directors also supervise both the internal and external audits of their Reserve Bank. For the external audit, the Federal Reserve Board appoints, sets compensation for, and evaluates the bank's external auditor. The directors do not oversee the Reserve Banks' supervisory activities of their member banks. The Reserve Banks' boards of directors use committees to help oversee the operations of the Reserve Banks and their branches. The Federal Reserve Board requires all Reserve Banks to have a standing audit committee and also, as needed, a search committee for the selection and appointment of a president. Various other committees are used by the Reserve Banks including budget and governance committees (app. III provides additional information on the committees at each of the Reserve Banks). Finally, directors serve as a link between the Federal Reserve System and private sector and the community.

According to Federal Reserve Board documents, this link is intended, in part, to provide the viewpoints of people with diverse backgrounds and experience that is useful in the formulation of national monetary policies and the oversight of Reserve Bank operations.

Financial Crisis and Federal Reserve Emergency Programs

The recent financial crisis that began around mid-2007 was the most severe that the United States has experienced since the Great Depression. A number of financial institutions were threatened with failure and some failed. The crisis also affected businesses and individuals, who found it increasingly difficult to obtain credit as cash-strapped banks held on to their assets. By late summer of 2008, the potential ramifications of the financial crisis included the continued failure of financial institutions, increased losses of individual wealth, reduced corporate investments, and further tightening of credit that would exacerbate the emerging global economic slowdown that was beginning to take shape.

Between late 2007 and early 2009, the Federal Reserve Board created more than a dozen new emergency programs to stabilize financial markets and authorized the Reserve Banks to provide financial assistance to avert the failures of a few individual institutions. In many cases, the decisions by the Federal Reserve Board, the FOMC, and the Reserve Banks about the authorization of, the initial terms of, and implementation of the Federal Reserve System's emergency assistance were made over the course of only days or weeks as the Federal Reserve Board sought to act quickly to address rapidly deteriorating market conditions. FRBNY implemented most of these emergency activities under authorization from the Federal Reserve Board. (See app. I for more information on the emergency programs and the Reserve Banks' involvement in their implementation).

Federal Reserve Bank Board Economic and Demographic Diversity Is Limited, and More Could be Done to Identify Diverse Candidates

According to the U.S. Census Bureau, the U.S. population has become more racially and ethnically diverse in the last 10 years. Between 2000 and

2010, the Asian population experienced the fastest rate of growth and the white population experienced the slowest rate of growth. In the 2010 Census, 97 percent of all respondents (299.7 million) reported only one race.[18] The largest group reported was white (223.6 million), accounting for 72 percent of all people living in the United States. The African-American population was 38.9 million and represented 13 percent of the total population. There were 2.9 million respondents who indicated American Indian and Alaska Native (0.9 percent). Approximately 14.7 million (about 5 percent of all respondents) identified their race as Asian. In 2010, there were 50.5 million Hispanics in the United States, composing 16 percent of the total population. Between 2000 and 2010, the Hispanic population grew by 43 percent—rising from 35.3 million in 2000, when this group made up 13 percent of the total population. The non-Hispanic population grew relatively slower over the decade, about 5 percent.

The Federal Reserve Act of 1913 as enacted did not include demographic diversity requirements. The act specified that the three Class A directors were to be chosen by and be representative of the stockholding banks. Further, the three Class B directors were to be actively engaged in their district in commerce, agriculture, or some other industrial pursuit, and the three Class C directors were appointed by the Federal Reserve Board. The Federal Reserve Reform Act of 1977 amended the Federal Reserve Act to add the present antidiscrimination requirements and to expand the economic diversity provisions to agriculture, commerce, industry, services, labor, and consumer representation for Class B and C directors.[19] According to the legislative history of the Reform Act, these changes were made to help broaden Reserve Bank board representation to include women and minorities, as well as industries and other interest groups.

The Federal Reserve Board maintains a database of current and past directors that is used to track demographic information voluntarily provided by directors. Information in this database is entered by the individual Reserve Banks and managed by the Federal Reserve Board. We analyzed demographic characteristics of bank (head office) and branch directors who served at some time during 2006 through 2010 to present a profile of director demographic characteristics.[20]

Figure 4 shows the representation of head office directors from 2006 through 2010 using Federal Reserve Board data. Over the 5-year period, we found that generally the representation of women and minority head office directors has remained limited. For example, in 2006, minorities accounted for

13 of 108 director positions; and in 2010 they accounted for 15 of 108 director positions. More specifically, in 2010, head office directors comprised 78 white men, 15 white women, 12 minority men, and 3 minority women.

We also analyzed the total number of female and minority directors serving from 2006 through 2010 by class.[21] As shown in figure 4, Class B and Class C directors were more diverse in gender, race, and ethnicity than Class A directors. For example, of the 202 directors serving from 2006 through 2010, 7 Class A directors were female, while there were approximately twice that number of female Class B and C directors, respectively—16 Class B and 16 Class C female directors. Furthermore, there were 3 minority Class A directors, while there were 14 minority Class B and 9 minority Class C directors. Several Reserve Bank officials we spoke with told us that Class B and Class C directors are a source of both economic and demographic diversity on Reserve Bank boards.

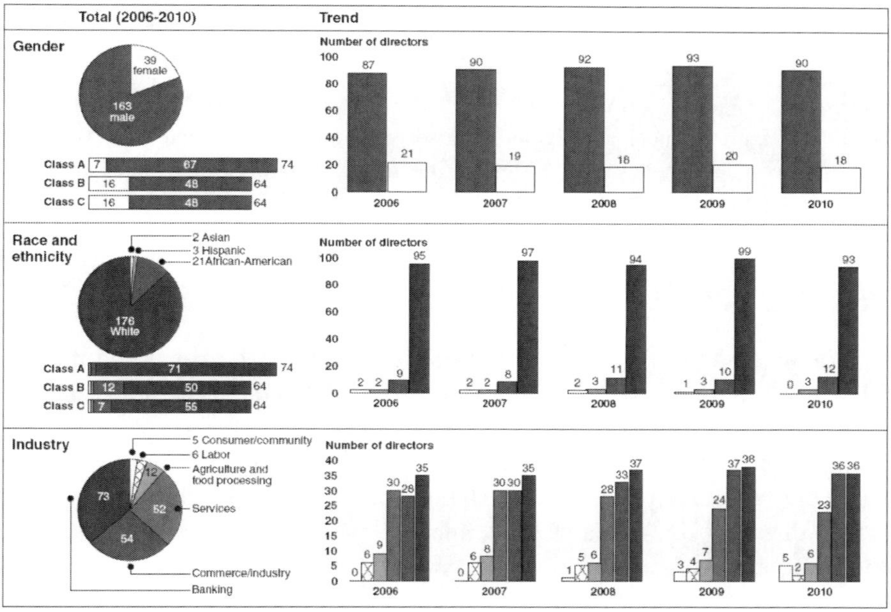

Source: Federal Reserve Board.

Note: The figure includes all directors that served during the calendar year. Directors who served multiple years during this time frame were removed to create a dataset of unique directors for the purposes of this analysis.

Figure 4. Trends in Federal Reserve Bank Head Office Directors by Gender, Race and Ethnicity, and Industry, 2006-2010.

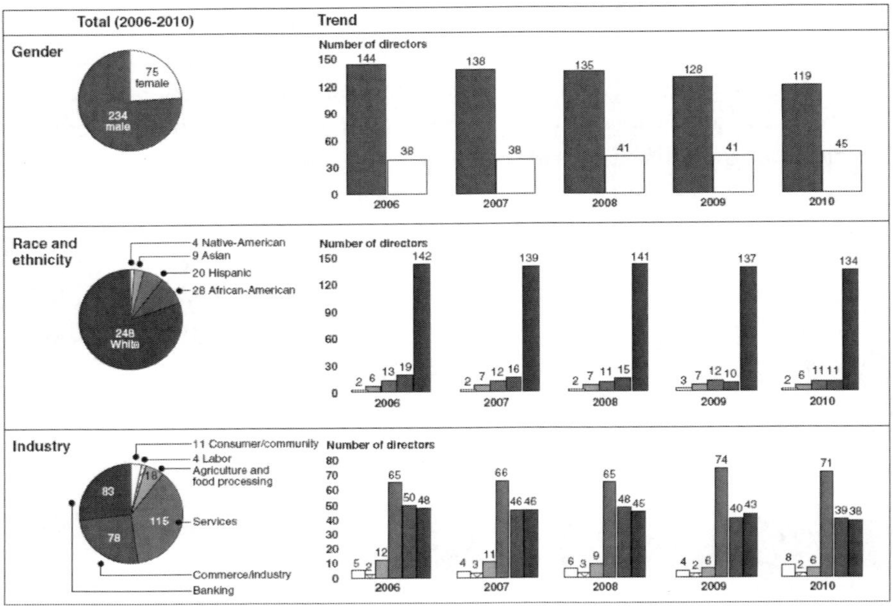

Source: Federal Reserve Board.

Note: The figure includes all directors that served during the calendar year. Directors who served multiple years during this time frame were removed to create a dataset of unique directors for the purposes of this analysis.

Figure 5. Trends in Federal Reserve Bank Branch Director Diversity by Gender, Race and Ethnicity, and Industry, 2006-2010.

Figure 5 shows the representation of branch directors from 2006 through 2010. Over the 5-year period we also found that generally, the representation of women and minority branch directors has also remained limited. For example, in 2006, minorities accounted for 40 of 182 director positions; and in 2010, they accounted for 30 of the 164 positions.[22] More specifically, in 2010, branch directors comprised 97 white men, 37 white women, 22 minority men, and 8 minority women.

The data show that labor and consumer groups are less represented than other industry groups on both head office and branch boards. As shown in figure 4, from 2006 through 2010, 5 of the 202 head office directors served as consumer representatives and 6 of the 202 head office directors served as labor representatives. As shown in figure 5, from 2006 through 2010, 11 of the 309 branch directors served as consumer representatives and 4 of the 309 branch directors served as labor representatives. The Federal Reserve Board has encouraged Reserve Banks to recruit directors from consumer and labor organizations. For example, in a February 2010 memo to Reserve Bank presidents on director recruitment, the Federal Reserve Board listed recruiting leaders from these two industry groups as a "high priority." Despite these efforts, two Reserve Bank officials we spoke with said recruiting consumer and labor representatives is a challenge because many of them are politically active and the Federal Reserve Board policy, which restricts a director's political activity, would generally require them to give up such activities while serving on the board.

As shown in figure 6, Federal Reserve Board data show that generally, representation of minority and female directors varied somewhat across districts. For example, of the 16 head office directors serving from 2006 through 2010 at both Federal Reserve Bank of Dallas and Federal Reserve Bank of Kansas City, 2 were women; and of the 18 head office directors serving from 2006 through 2010 at Federal Reserve Bank of Boston, 5 were women. One Reserve Bank corporate secretary we spoke with said that it was difficult to recruit diverse candidates within his district because of a lack of overall diversity in the region.

Survey of Directors Shows That More Than Half Have Financial Experience

To obtain information from all current directors on a cross section of high-level issues, we conducted a web-based survey of the 105 Reserve Bank directors that served for the full year during 2010.[23] We collected and summarized additional demographic information for 2010 directors, such as their prior work experience, education, and other board positions. Many Reserve Bank directors responding to the survey typically had experience in the finance industry and almost all currently serve on a variety of other boards. At least 56 have had some financial industry experience.[24] After the financial industry, the next most reported work experiences by industry were manufacturing; professional, scientific, and technical services; retail trade; and real estate and rental leasing.[25] The vast majority of the directors who responded to the survey reported that they had completed a bachelor's degree. More specifically, over half of the directors responding to the survey (55) reported that they had completed some type of advanced degree, such as a master's, juris doctor, or doctorate. In 2010, 86 of 91 Reserve Bank directors responding to our survey served on a variety of nonprofit, private, and public company boards. For example, directors held board positions at public and private universities; for-profit companies such as Loews Corporation, Safeway, Inc., and Energizer Holdings; and nonprofit organizations such as the Ford Foundation and Ronald McDonald House Charities.

Reserve Bank Directors Are Generally Senior Executives, a Subset of Management That Is Less Diverse

We analyzed EEOC's EEO-1 data for employers with 100 or more employees from 2007 through 2009. The EEO-1 data provide information on racial/ethnic and gender representation for various occupations within a broad range of industries. We used the EEO-1 "executive and senior level officials and managers" job category as the basis for our analysis because this is the category of employees from which Reserve Banks would most likely recruit directors. EEOC defines the job category of executive and senior level officials and managers as individuals residing in the highest levels of organizations who plan, direct, and formulate policies, and provide overall direction for the development and delivery of products and services. Figure 7 provides EEO-1 data for individual minority groups and illustrates their trend in representation at the management level, which varied by group.

As shown in figure 7, among all EEO-1 reporters, senior management representation by whites and Asians increased from 2007 through 2009. For example, whites accounted for 87.4 percent of all industry senior management positions in 2007; and they accounted for 88.6 percent of senior managers in 2009. Moreover, while representation by Asians also increased during this period, African Americans and Hispanics in senior management decreased steadily. For example, Hispanics accounted for 4.5 percent of all industry senior management positions in 2007; and they accounted for 3.5 percent in 2009. Representation for "Other" races remained constant from 2007 through 2009.

Figure 7 also compares race and ethnicity and gender between the EEO- 1 and Federal Reserve Board datasets. EEO-1 data show that the pool of senior managers—a possible pipeline for potential Federal Reserve directors—has limited diversity. For example, minorities accounted for 12.6 percent of all senior management positions in 2007 and 11.4 percent in 2009. Similarly, minorities accounted for 12.4 percent of Federal Reserve directors in 2009.

Gender (percentage)	Men	Women	White %	White Number	Asian %	Asian Number	Hispanic %	Hispanic Number	African-American %	African-American Number
Boston	72.2	27.8	88.9	16	0	0	0	0	11.1	2
New York	81.3	18.8	87.5	14	6.3	1	6.3	1	0	0
Philadelphia	82.4	17.6	88.2	15	0	0	0	0	11.8	2
Cleveland	75.0	25.0	87.5	14	0	0	0	0	12.5	2
Richmond	76.5	23.5	88.2	15	0	0	0	0	11.8	2
Atlanta	77.8	22.2	83.3	15	0	0	0	0	16.7	3
Chicago	84.2	15.8	89.5	17	0	0	0	0	10.5	2
St. Louis	81.3	18.8	93.8	15	0	0	0	0	6.3	1
Minneapolis	88.9	11.1	88.9	16	0	0	0	0	11.1	2
Kansas City	87.5	12.5	93.8	15	0	0	6.3	1	0	0
Dallas	87.5	12.5	81.3	13	0	0	6.3	1	12.5	2
San Francisco	73.3	26.7	73.3	11	6.7	1	0	0	20.0	3

Race and ethnicity (percentage)

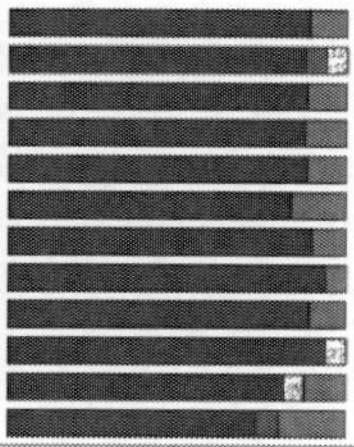

Source: Federal Reserve Board.

Note: The figure includes all directors that served during the calendar year. Directors who served multiple years during this time frame were removed to create a dataset of unique directors for the purposes of this analysis.

Figure 6. Federal Reserve Data on Head Office Directors' Gender and Race and Ethnicity by Federal Reserve District, 2006-2010.

Gender (percentage)		Men	Women	White %	White Number	Asian %	Asian Number	Hispanic %	Hispanic Number	African-American %	African-American Number	Other[a] %	Other[a] Number
2007	Directors	82.6%	17.4	89.0	97	1.8	2	1.8	2	7.3	8	NA	NA
	EEO	71.4	28.6	87.4	788,107	3.7	33,368	4.5	40,202	3.6	32,146	0.9	7,661
2008	Directors	83.6	16.4	85.5	94	1.8	2	2.7	3	10.0	11	NA	NA
	EEO	71.0	29.0	88.0	767,735	3.9	34,139	3.8	32,963	3.4	29,627	0.9	7,922
2009	Directors	82.3	17.7	87.6	99	0.9	1	2.7	3	8.9	10	NA	NA
	EEO	71.7	28.3	88.6	711,504	4.0	32,296	3.5	28,047	3.0	24,447	0.9	7,055

Race and ethnicity (percentage)

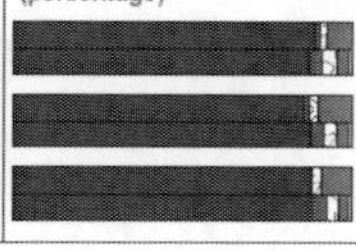

Source: Federal Reserve Board and Equal Employment Opportunity Commission.

Notes: Beginning in 2007, EEOC started to collect separate data on "executive/senior level officials and managers," which includes individuals who reside in the highest levels of organizations and plan, direct, and formulate policies, set strategy; and provide the overall direction of enterprises/organizations for the development and delivery of products or services, within the parameters approved by boards of directors or other governing bodies. For the Reserve Banks, data include all directors that served during the calendar year. Directors who served multiple years during this time frame were removed to create a dataset of unique directors for the purposes of this analysis.

[a] "Other" is defined as anyone who selected "American Indian," "Hawaiian or Pacific Islander," or "Two or more races."

Figure 7. Comparison of EEO-1 and Head Office Federal Reserve Diversity Data by Gender and Race and Ethnicity, 2007-2009.

As shown in figure 8, diversity was limited among senior-level management in the commercial banking industry. Because Class A directors are nominated and elected by the member banks in each Federal Reserve district to represent the stockholding banks, they are generally officers or directors of a member commercial bank.[26] EEO-1 data show that, on average, the pool of senior managers in the commercial banking industry, a source that provides the pool of candidates for Class A directors, is less diverse than senior management in terms of race and ethnicity in all other industries combined. In 2009, the percentage of senior management positions held by minorities ranged from an average of 9.6 percent for commercial banking institutions to an average of 11.5 percent for all other industries combined. However, the average percentage of positions held by women was relatively consistent between commercial banking institutions and all other industries, 29.0 percent and 28.3 percent, respectively.

Reserve Bank officials said they generally focus their search on senior executives. To explore whether Reserve Banks expanding their search to include nonexecutives would increase diversity, we spoke with officials and directors about their views on this matter. Several Reserve Bank executives and directors told us that having senior executives on the board of directors helps elevate the stature of the board. In addition, they said that individuals working at the top of their organization may have a broader view of how their industry is being affected by the economy. On the other hand, one Reserve Bank official told us that he felt looking below the executive level for potential directors was important. Further, at one Reserve Bank, the corporate secretary told us the bank actively looks for directors who may not be senior-level executives in an attempt to increase diversity. At another Reserve Bank, the corporate secretary stated that the bank has had nonexecutives serve on the board both currently and in the past.

In previous work on diversity in the financial services industry, we found that individuals holding positions one level below senior management were more diverse than senior management.[27] According to this work, EEOC data showed that generally, management-level representation by minority women and men increased from 11.1 percent to 17.4 percent from 1993 through 2008. However, these EEOC data overstated minority representation at senior management levels, because the category included midlevel management positions, such as assistant branch manager, that may have greater minority representation. In 2008, EEOC reported revised data for senior-level positions only, which showed that minorities held 10 percent of such positions compared with 17.4 percent of all management positions. This suggests that by broadening its pool of potential candidates below the executive level, Reserve

Banks may be able to attract more diverse director candidates with potentially more diverse backgrounds and perspectives on the economy.

We also analyzed EEO-1 data by Federal Reserve district to determine district-level trends in senior management across all industries. This analysis demonstrates that diversity of senior managers in the Federal Reserve districts varies. As shown in figure 9, certain Federal Reserve districts' territories are somewhat more diverse than others at the senior management level. For example, in 2009, the percentage of senior management positions held by minorities ranged from a high of 18.7 percent within the Federal Reserve Bank of San Francisco's territory to a low of 4.0 percent within the Federal Reserve Bank of Minneapolis territory, indicating that diversity among senior managers does vary by district.

Year	Sector	Gender (percentage) Men	Women	Race and ethnicity (percentage) White	Asian	Hispanic	African-American	Other[a]
2007	Other	71.5	28.5	87.4	3.7	4.5	3.6	0.9
	Banking	69.1	30.9	89.7	3.7	3.3	2.8	0.5
2008	Other	71.1	28.9	87.9	3.9	3.8	3.4	0.9
	Banking	70.0	30.0	90.4	3.3	3.1	2.6	0.7
2009	Other	71.7	28.3	88.5	4.0	3.5	3.1	0.9
	Banking	71.1	29.0	90.4	3.3	3.1	2.6	0.7

Source: Equal Employment Opportunity Commission.

Note: Prior to 2007 the two job categories "executive/senior level officials and managers" and "first/mid-level officials and managers" were grouped together.

Figure 8. Trends in EEO-1 Data by Gender and Race and Ethnicity for Banking Compared with Other Industries at the Senior Management Level by Banking and Nonbanking Sectors, 2007 through 2009.

District	Gender (percentage) Men	Women	Race and ethnicity (percentage) White	Asian	Hispanic	African-American	Other[a]
Boston	70.8	29.2	94.3	2.5	1.5	1.3	0.4
New York	69.2	30.8	86.7	5.7	3.4	3.6	0.6
Philadelphia	72.8	27.2	92.5	2.3	1.7	3.0	0.5
Cleveland	72.3	27.8	93.4	2.4	1.3	2.7	0.4
Richmond	71.6	28.4	88.8	2.8	2.1	5.6	0.8
Atlanta	72.1	29.7	87.0	2.0	5.5	4.8	0.7
Chicago	72.3	27.7	92.9	2.7	2.0	2.8	0.5
St. Louis	73.0	27.0	93.2	1.3	1.6	3.3	0.6
Minneapolis	69.3	30.8	96.0	1.3	1.1	0.9	0.7
Kansas City	72.0	28.0	91.9	1.4	3.6	1.6	1.6
Dallas	75.4	24.6	86.5	2.7	7.1	2.8	0.9
San Francisco	71.3	28.8	81.3	9.6	5.4	1.9	1.9

Source: Equal Employment Opportunity Commission.

Figure 9. EEO-1 Data by Gender, Race and Ethnicity for all Industries at the Senior Management Level by Federal Reserve District Territories, 2009.

Reserve Banks Identify Potential Directors in a Variety of Ways, Often Relying on Networking

Reserve Banks select candidates to fill director vacancies based upon criteria in the Federal Reserve Act and guidance from the Federal Reserve Board. The act provides requirements for the nomination and election of directors. The act requires that member banks of each district be classified into three groups consisting of banks of similar capitalization—small, medium, and large. The member banks in each group nominate and elect one Class A director to represent that group's banks and one Class B director to represent the public. After the candidates are identified and a list of their names is forwarded to the member banks, each bank may cast one vote for a Class A director and one vote for a Class B director. Class C directors, who also represent the public, are recommended by the Reserve Banks and appointed by the Federal Reserve Board. The Federal Reserve Board also provides guidance on director election and eligibility requirements in the *Federal Reserve Administrative Manual* (FRAM).[28] Additionally, the act specifies that all directors shall be chosen without discrimination as to race, creed, color, sex, or national origin and that Class B and Class C directors who represent the public shall be elected "with due but not exclusive consideration to the interests of agriculture, commerce, industry, services, labor, and consumers." Each year the Federal Reserve Board provides a memorandum to Reserve Banks with priority objectives for the recruitment of individuals with independent and diverse views and potential sources from which to obtain diverse directors. In addition, it distributes a yearly report on the demographic and industry characteristics of directors to each of the Reserve Banks for their use as they seek to identify and consider potential candidates.

Reserve Banks review the current demographics and areas of expertise of their boards when selecting candidates to fill director vacancies. At each Reserve Bank, the corporate secretary works collaboratively with the president and other senior bank staff to assess the demographics of their board and identify areas where additional representation may be needed. Several Reserve Bank officials with whom we spoke told us they also consider geography and educational background as selection criteria, in addition to those outlined in the act. Three Reserve Bank officials told us that while they strive to find diverse candidates from a variety of industries, they also want to find people who have the skills and knowledge that will fill a gap in the board's existing knowledge and skill set. Additionally, Reserve Bank officials said they generally focus their search on senior executives, usually chief executive officers (CEO) or presidents. For example, of the 108 directors serving in 2010, 82 were the president or CEO of their company. Further, we identified at least 23 who were employed by Fortune 500 companies in 2010.[29] Three Reserve Bank officials we spoke with indicated that CEOs generally have a better familiarity with the economic and business community of their district than less senior managers. However, as discussed previously, while having executives on the boards may elevate the stature of the board, it may limit the diversity of the pool of potential candidates.

Reserve Banks identify potential director candidates in a variety of ways and often use different recruitment methods. In general, Reserve Banks use a combination of personal networking and community outreach efforts to identify potential candidates. Two directors with whom we spoke told us they have recommended personal or business acquaintances they believe would be qualified to serve as directors. In addition, some Reserve Banks contact former directors for help in identifying possible candidates. Several Reserve Bank presidents and senior staff also attend community roundtables and forums to network and identify potential candidates. Several Reserve Banks use their advisory councils and branch boards as a source for potential candidates. One Reserve Bank official told us that they look for candidates in a variety of industry lists such as a Forbes' magazine list of the most powerful women in business. At another Reserve Bank, member banks of the states represented in the district have agreed to a rotating nomination process for Class A and Class B directors to help ensure geographic representation. That is, when it is one particular state's turn to nominate a candidate, the state's Banking Association identifies potential candidates. At least one Class C director said he self-identified for the position and approached the Reserve Bank to express his interest in serving on the board when a vacancy came up.

Some Reserve Banks also use nominating committees to identify qualified director candidates. These committees may do so by recruiting candidates to fill vacant seats on the board, reviewing candidates recommended by the Reserve Banks and others, or conducting inquiries into the backgrounds and qualifications of potential candidates. Five Reserve Banks use nominating committees to identify potential candidates. For example, one Reserve Bank has a nominating committee that considers candidates for the Federal Reserve Board-appointed Class C directors. At another Reserve Bank, the nominating committee currently consists of three Class C directors and two Class A directors that meet to consider and make recommendations concerning board membership for all classes of directors. Guidelines in the FRAM require that nominating committees recommending Class A and Class B director candidates not include Reserve Bank officers and employees.

Typically, a Reserve Bank identifies and vets potential candidates for Class A and B directors, and communicates their names and credentials to member banks for their nomination and election. Reserve Banks generally submit an open call for nominations to the district's voting banks, even if they also have a nominating committee. Typically, the member banks will elect the Class A and B candidates identified and vetted by the Reserve Bank's nominating committee. However, member banks can nominate and elect a candidate that has not been vetted by the Reserve Bank. In such cases, the bank will inform the nominee of a director's eligibility requirements, to determine if the candidate is eligible to serve, if elected. We found that member bank voter turnout was often low at some Reserve Banks. Although the Federal Reserve Act sets forth specific procedures and voting requirements for director elections, shareholder elections of Reserve Bank directors do not have a requirement for a minimum number of votes.

The Federal Reserve Board requires every Reserve Bank to provide a slate of at least two candidates for each Class C vacancy to the Federal Reserve Board for appointment. Typically, the Federal Reserve Board will appoint a candidate from the slate provided by the Reserve Banks to serve as a Class C director. However, the Federal Reserve Board may ask for further explanation of why Reserve Banks selected certain candidates or ask for alternative candidates.

Several Reserve Banks indicated that recruiting directors for several groups—specifically women, minority, and labor or consumer representatives—can be challenging. According to Reserve Bank officials, recruiting labor and consumer representatives is particularly difficult because many of them are politically active and the Federal Reserve Board policy generally restricts a director's political activity. They also noted that Reserve Bank directors' roles and responsibilities can be time consuming and that compensation is low compared with that available in other opportunities to serve on private boards. [30] After the passage of the Sarbanes-Oxley Act in 2002, directors are limited in the number of public company boards on which they can serve; therefore, Reserve Banks compete with other private corporations for these directors' time, especially women and minorities.[31] In addition, some individuals do not want to divest of their stock holdings in the banking- related industry (which would be required for Class C) and also may not wish to refrain from political participation, according to Federal Reserve System officials.

As we have previously reported, many private and public organizations have recognized the importance of recruiting and retaining minority and women candidates for key positions as the U.S. workforce has become increasingly diverse. Some Reserve Bank officials told us that many organizations are searching for diverse directors to have on their boards, and the Reserve Banks are competing with private corporations for the same small pool of qualified individuals. Although the policies of private corporate boards we reviewed do not have specific requirements for board diversity, the Securities and Exchange Commission (SEC) recently started requiring companies to identify steps taken to ensure diversity of their boards in their proxy statement to shareholders. In our review of the proxy statements from the 10 largest bank holding companies in 2010, we found that companies generally did not list specific steps taken to identify and select diverse board members (see app. IV for a list of the 10 largest bank holding companies included in our review). Rather they provided a broad statement about diversity. For example, one company stated, "The [Nominating] Committee evaluates diversity in a broad sense, recognizing the benefits of racial and gender diversity, but also considering the breadth of backgrounds, skills, and experiences that directors and candidates may bring to our Board."

Having a demographically and economically diverse board strengthens an organization by bringing a wider variety of perspectives and approaches to the organization. While officials at some Reserve Banks told us they consider candidates who are not chief-level executives (i.e., not chief financial officers, chief operating officers, or executive vice presidents), the vast majority of directors in 2010 held such positions in their organizations. By broadening their pool of candidates, Reserve Banks may be able to improve diversity, and ultimately public representation, on the Reserve Bank boards. Such diversification can help ensure that the Federal Reserve System receives a broader spectrum of information useful for the formation and execution of monetary policy and the oversight of Reserve Bank operations.

ADDITIONAL STEPS NEEDED TO MANAGE DIRECTORS' ACTUAL OR POTENTIAL CONFLICTS OF INTEREST AND OUTSIDE AFFILIATIONS

From the creation of the Federal Reserve System, the Federal Reserve Act has required the Reserve Banks to include Class A directors on their boards to be representative of the member banks, as each of the Reserve Banks is owned by the member banks in its district. While Class A directors are not required to be officers or employees of member banks, in practice, most Class A directors are officers or directors of member banks in the district. The requirement to have representatives of member banks creates an appearance of a conflict of interest because, as noted previously, the Federal Reserve System has supervisory authority over state-chartered member banks and bank holding companies. Conflicts of interest involving directors have been historically addressed through both federal law and Federal Reserve System policies and procedures, such as by defining roles and responsibilities and implementing codes of conduct to identify, manage, and mitigate potential conflicts. Nevertheless, directors' affiliations with financial firms and former directors' business relationships with Reserve Banks continue to pose reputational risks to the Federal Reserve System. When the Federal Reserve System played a key role in providing assistance to financial institutions during the 2007-2009 financial crisis, Reserve Bank board governance came under scrutiny because, among other things, a number of director-affiliated banks and nonbank financial institutions participated in the Federal Reserve System's emergency programs. Since then, Congress, the Federal Reserve Board, and Reserve Banks have made a number of changes to the policies and procedures that address Reserve Bank governance. However, without more complete documentation of the directors' roles and responsibilities with regard to the supervision and regulation functions, as well as increased public disclosure on governance practices to enhance accountability and transparency, questions about Reserve Bank governance will remain.

Some Directors' Affiliations Can Expose Reserve Banks to Reputational Risk

The three classes of Reserve Bank directors have varying degrees of involvement in the financial services industry, and their affiliations with financial companies could create reputational risk for the Reserve Banks. In addition, relationships between current and former directors and interactions between former directors and the Reserve Banks could also raise questions about the independence of the directors and actions of the Reserve Banks. Finally, questions about directors' involvement in the emergency programs authorized by the Federal Reserve Board during the financial crisis spurred allegations of conflicts of interest. As we reported in our July 2010 report on the emergency programs, our review found that the boards of directors generally were not directly involved in the development and implementation of emergency programs.[32]

Directors' Affiliations with Financial Firms

Federal Reserve Bank directors often serve on the boards of a variety of financial firms as well as those of nonprofit, private, and public companies. For example, in 2010, 86 of 91 Reserve Bank directors responding to our survey held board positions at public and private companies, public and private universities, and nonprofit organizations. As noted earlier, our survey indicated that most of the Reserve Banks have directors who have held positions at financial services firms or insurance companies as well as banks. This includes Class A directors who are officials of banks that hold stock in the Reserve Bank, and Class C directors, who are required by the Federal Reserve Act to be persons of tested banking experience, which the Federal Reserve Board says has come to be interpreted as requiring familiarity with banking or financial services. In addition, as the financial services industry has evolved, more companies are involved in financial services or otherwise interconnected with financial institutions. These changes have resulted in a few Class B and Class C directors who were previously employed by financial institutions or have served on their boards.

A recent example that raised questions about affiliations, and the nature of director affiliations with financial firms, involved the then-FRBNY chairman in late 2008, who was former chairman and a current board member and shareholder of the Goldman Sachs Group, Inc. (Goldman Sachs). As illustrated in figure 10, when the then-FRBNY chairman joined the FRBNY board as a Class C director in January 2008, Goldman Sachs was an investment bank outside the supervisory authority of the Federal Reserve System. However, in September 2008, in response to the unfolding financial crisis, Goldman Sachs applied for and was approved by the Federal Reserve Board to become a bank holding company. As a result, under Federal Reserve Board policy, the then-FRBNY chairman became ineligible to serve as a Class C director because he was then a director and stockholder of a bank holding company.[33] Without consultation with the full FRBNY board, FRBNY sought a waiver to allow the then-FRBNY chairman to continue to serve on the board. According to an FRBNY official, FRBNY sought the waiver in October 2008 for a number of reasons. First, finding a new chairman during the financial crisis would have been difficult, given that FRBNY already had one director vacancy on its board at the time. Further, the event leading to the need for a waiver was unexpected and unforeseen. In late November 2008, an additional concern was raised that the then-FRBNY president was expected to be nominated as the Secretary of the Treasury, thereby raising the potential that FRBNY would be searching for both a new president and a new chairman simultaneously, with the added complication that, as the chair of the FRBNY board, the then-FRBNY chairman would be heading the search committee for a new president. The waiver was granted by the Federal Reserve Board in January 2009 on the basis of these considerations. However, the Federal Reserve Board was unaware that the then-FRBNY chairman had purchased additional shares in Goldman Sachs via an automatic stock purchase program. The then-FRBNY chair resigned in May 2009. As discussed later, on the basis of this waiver experience, the Federal Reserve Board decided to develop and institute a formal policy governing the treatment of situations in which Class B or C directors' stockholdings unexpectedly become impermissible. This policy has since been adopted. FRBNY also changed its policy, which would require that waivers be discussed by the board of directors before going to the Federal Reserve Board.

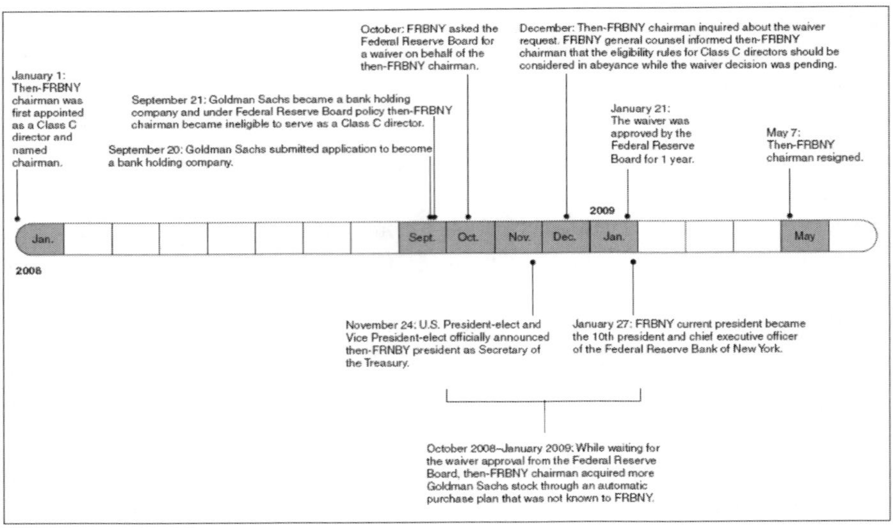

Source: GAO's presentation of information from FRBNY and then-FRBNY chairman's legal representative.

Figure 10. Effect of Goldman-Sachs's Transition to a Bank Holding Company on FRBNY Board, from January 1, 2008, through May 7, 2009.

Federal Reserve Board officials told us that after receiving the waiver request from FRBNY, they contacted other Reserve Bank boards to determine whether any other directors held stocks in companies that had recently converted to bank holding companies. According to these officials, this review identified a director from the Federal Reserve Bank of Minneapolis who held less than $100,000 in stock in Merrill Lynch & Co., Inc., an investment bank, which had been acquired by Bank of America, a bank holding company. This director remained on the board and a waiver was granted by the Federal Reserve Board, but nonetheless, he subsequently divested the shares in January 2009.

Another situation that raised questions about affiliations involved a FRBNY Class B director. The director was the Chief Executive Officer of Lehman Brothers Holdings, Inc. (Lehman), an investment bank that experienced significant financial problems during the unfolding financial crisis and ultimately failed. An FRBNY official said that he met with the FRBNY president and chairman about Lehman's deteriorating financial condition, without the full board, and concluded that FRBNY faced reputational risk regardless of the action taken. Specifically, it was concluded that although the board of directors was not involved in approving and implementing the emergency programs, a recusal from board meetings by the Lehman director might not have managed the appearance of a conflict and a public resignation might have sent a negative signal to the market and hastened the collapse of the firm. Under Federal Reserve Board practice, Reserve Bank directors affiliated with troubled financial institutions are encouraged to resign or risk removal from the board. Federal Reserve System officials said that the director voluntarily resigned before Lehman filed for bankruptcy.

Although directors' affiliations with financial firms do not necessarily create conflicts of interest, they may complicate the directors' relationships with the Reserve Banks and increase public scrutiny of them. One issue relates to directors' communications with Reserve Bank officials in their roles as senior executives of their companies. These situations have raised questions as to whether directors have greater access to Reserve Bank officials than other financial institution officials and whether they have influence over matters that may affect banks or institutions with which they are affiliated. Reserve Bank officials with whom we spoke said that there are no restrictions on directors communicating with Reserve Bank staff about their respective banks or holding companies in their capacity as officials of the bank nor are there restrictions on conversations about the financial markets. However, according to Federal Reserve Board officials, members of the Reserve Bank board of directors are not granted special access to supervisory staff, and it has been the practice of the Federal Reserve Board and the Reserve Banks to restrict their involvement in supervision issues. Further, Reserve Bank officials said that requests from other financial institutions to meet with Reserve Bank staff are processed in the same manner as those from the directors. As discussed later, the financial crisis highlighted situations where directors were in contact with Reserve Bank staff in their capacity as representatives of their financial institutions and market participants.

Interconnections among Current Directors, Former Directors and the Reserve Banks Have Raised Questions

After completing their terms, directors who had represented member banks or who have affiliations with other financial institutions may maintain contact with Federal Reserve Bank officials for various reasons. FRBNY officials said that actions such as the Reserve Banks' management of such communications may help safeguard against improprieties. For example, during the 2008 financial crisis, the company of a former FRBNY director was negotiating with FRBNY regarding assets the Reserve Bank had acquired when it extended credit against the assets of Bear Stearns Companies, Inc. The former director felt that there was a miscommunication and contacted a number of FRBNY staff he knew to discuss the issue. The director's preexisting relationship with FRBNY raised questions about the appropriateness of FRBNY's actions in its negotiations with the former director's firm. Recently, FRBNY implemented a procedure to document contacts involving directors by reporting calls and their content in a memo to the chairman of the board's Audit and Operational Risk Committee.

Reserve Bank officials said that many of the Reserve Banks maintain programs to keep in touch with former directors. These can be formal programs such as annual holiday functions or informal ways to continue to seek former directors' views on the economy and their industries. Reserve Bank officials described these contacts as "unobjectionable." A former Federal Reserve Board governor with whom we spoke also thought that these contacts are appropriate. As discussed later, indirect connections between directors' firms and Reserve Banks when the firms used the emergency programs or acted as service providers have also raised questions.

Reserve Bank Boards of Directors Generally Were Not Involved in the Development and Implementation of Emergency Programs

The Federal Reserve Board, and in some cases, the FOMC, authorized the creation and modification of most of the emergency programs under authorities granted by the Federal Reserve Act.[34] Although a number of Reserve Bank directors were affiliated with institutions that borrowed from the emergency programs, we did not find evidence that Reserve Bank boards of directors participated directly in making any decisions about authorizing, setting the terms of, or approving a borrower's participation in the emergency programs.

Our review did not reveal that Reserve Bank directors received nonpublic information on the emergency programs. A review of minutes from the 12 Reserve Bank board meetings during the unfolding crisis revealed that discussions of emergency programs during board meetings appeared to have occurred after the emergency programs had been publicly announced. Further, presentations by Reserve Bank staff generally covered explanations of the related emergency lending authority, administration of the program, descriptive information about the programs' operations and risks, and the impact on the Reserve Banks' balance sheets. Moreover, Federal Reserve Board officials and Reserve Bank directors from all 12 Reserve Banks with whom we spoke told us that the Reserve Bank boards did not play a role in the creation or implementation of the emergency programs. Federal Reserve Board officials also pointed out that all Reserve Bank directors are prohibited from disclosing nonpublic information related to the programs and such disclosures may risk violating insider trading laws.

While all Reserve Banks implemented the Term Auction Facility, FRBNY implemented the majority of the emergency programs.[35] A number of FRBNY's directors played a limited oversight role as prescribed in a written Audit and Operational Risk Committee (AORC) protocol that states the oversight by the directors was focused on operational risks. For example, according to FRBNY officials, FRBNY staff periodically briefed the committee on the composition of an asset portfolio that was created to assist Bear Stearns when it was near failure to help ensure that the directors were aware of how the bank was managing certain high-risk assets. FRBNY has five directors on the audit committee. During the financial crisis, at least one Class A director served on this committee at any given time. According to FRBNY officials, to help ensure that one class of directors does not have undue influence, FRBNY strengthened its governance structure by revising its AORC charter to permit only two out of five committee members to be Class A directors.[36] Although implemented after the unwinding of many of the emergency programs, the enhanced standards helped mitigate the appearance of actual and potential director conflicts by ensuring that Class A directors are not the majority on the AORC. Appendix III provides more information on the Reserve Bank committees.

As mentioned earlier, in their role as market participants, some FRBNY directors were consulted by FRBNY management and staff as certain emergency facilities were being created. According to FRBNY officials, a director providing information to FRBNY management and staff in his or her role as chief executive officer of an institution does not equate to "participating personally and substantially"—as defined by 18 U.S.C. § 208, discussed below—because the director is not playing a direct role with respect to approving a program or providing a recommendation. According to FRBNY officials, FRBNY's Capital Markets Group contacted representatives from primary dealers, commercial paper issuers, and other institutions to gain a sense of how to design and calibrate some of the emergency programs. For example, FRBNY officials said that General Electric Company (General Electric), whose chief executive officer was serving as a Class B director at the time, was one of the largest issuers of commercial paper and General Electric was one of the companies FRBNY consulted when creating the emergency program to assist with the commercial paper market. FRBNY officials said they contacted institutions for this purpose irrespective of whether one of FRBNY's directors was affiliated with the institution.

Some of the institutions that borrowed from the emergency programs had senior executives and stockholders that served on Reserve Banks' board of directors. These relationships contributed to questions about Reserve Bank governance and also raised concerns about conflicts of interest. We identified at least 18 former and current Class A, B, and C directors from 9 Reserve Banks who were affiliated with institutions that used at least one emergency program. In those cases, 11 Class A directors who served between 2008 and 2010 worked for member banks that used an emergency program. There are 2 Class B directors who served between 2008 and 2010 and worked for companies that used an emergency program. Similarly, one Class C director who served between 2008 and 2009 was affiliated with a company that used at least one program. In addition, there are 4 former Class A directors who served between 2006 and 2007 whose companies used the emergency facilities. The Term Auction Facility was the most commonly used facility.

According to Federal Reserve Board officials, the Federal Reserve Board allowed borrowers to access its emergency programs only if they satisfied publicly announced eligibility criteria. Thus, Reserve Banks granted access to borrowing institutions affiliated with Reserve Bank directors only if these institutions satisfied the proper criteria, regardless of potential director-affiliated outreach or whether the institution was affiliated with a director. As we reported in our July report, our analysis did not find evidence indicating a systemic bias toward favoring one or more eligible institutions.[37] While some institutions that borrowed from these programs were affiliated with a Reserve Bank director, these institutions were subject to the same terms and conditions as those that had no such affiliation.

As another example, the Chief Executive Officer of JP Morgan Chase & Co. (JP Morgan Chase) served on the FRBNY board of directors at the same time that his bank participated in various emergency programs and served as one of the clearing banks for emergency lending programs. According to Federal Reserve Board officials, there are only two entities, including JP Morgan Chase, that offer services as clearing banks for triparty repurchase agreements and both banks served as clearing banks for the emergency programs.[38] Similarly, Lehman's Chief Executive Officer served on the FRBNY board while Lehman's broker-dealer subsidiary participated in emergency programs such as the Primary Dealer Credit Facility.[39]

Existing Policies and Procedures to Manage and Mitigate Actual and Potential Conflicts of Interest Involving Directors

Having the Class A directors, who represent member banks, and the Class B directors, who are elected by member banks, as required by the Federal Reserve Act, creates an appearance of a conflict of interest. This is because Class A or B directors might own stock in banks or Class A directors might work for banks that are supervised by the Reserve Bank while also overseeing aspects of the Reserve Banks' operations, including the bank presidents' evaluation and salary and personnel decisions for the supervision and regulation function.[40] In addition, Class B directors are involved in the president selection process. In turn, the president oversees the supervision and regulation function, which regulates the member banks that vote for the Class A and B directors. The president also may serve on the FOMC.

Conflicts of interest involving directors have been historically addressed through both federal law and Federal Reserve System policies and procedures.

First, individuals serving on the boards of directors of the Reserve Banks are generally subject to the federal criminal conflict-of- interest restrictions in section 208 of title 18 of the U.S. Code and its implementing regulations. 18 U.S.C. § 208 generally prohibits Reserve Bank directors from participating personally and substantially in their official capacities in any matter in which, to their knowledge, they have a financial interest, if the particular matter will have a direct and predictable effect on that interest.[41] The Office of Government Ethics regulations implementing 18 U.S.C. § 208 include provisions concerning divestiture, disqualification (recusal), and waivers or exemptions from disqualification.[42] The regulations also provide that Reserve Bank directors may participate in specified matters, even though they may be particular matters in which they have a disqualifying financial interest. These matters concern the establishment of rates to be charged to member banks for all advances and discounts; consideration of monetary policy matters and other matters of broad applicability; and approval or ratification of extensions of credit, advances or discounts to healthy depository institutions, or in certain conditions, to depository institutions in hazardous condition.[43] As the rulemaking for these exemptions notes, because of their ties to the financial services industry and their communities, it is likely that at least some directors will have financial conflicts with their duties, and the exemptions adopted by the Office of Government Ethics were necessary to resolve any possible conflict between the directors' statutorily mandated function and the performance of their official duties.[44]

The Federal Reserve Board and Reserve Banks have policies and procedures to identify, manage, and mitigate conflicts of interest that could result from a Reserve Bank director having financial or other interests that conflict with the interests of the Reserve Bank. These steps include defining the roles and responsibilities of directors to avoid conflicts, managing and mitigating conflicts of interest through adherence to federal law and the Federal Reserve board's conflict-of-interest policies, and establishing internal controls and policies to identify and manage potential conflicts.

Roles and Responsibilities

The Federal Reserve Board, within the requirements of the Federal Reserve Act, defines Reserve Bank directors' overall roles and responsibilities. In doing so, it manages and mitigates conflicts with respect to directors' involvement with bank supervision and regulation by precluding director involvement in institution-specific supervision matters and establishes restrictions on directors' interaction with the Reserve Banks' supervision and regulation function. Additionally the Federal Reserve Board monitors the performance of the Supervision and Regulation Department of the Reserve Banks. Actual or potential conflicts of interest could arise if directors were consulted about supervisory matters because of their stock ownership or affiliation with the supervised entity or with a competitor or customer of the supervised entity. Our analysis of the board minutes, interviews, and survey of Reserve Bank directors reveals that interaction between the directors and the supervision and regulation staff was generally limited and that the directors were not involved in the day-to-day operations of supervision and regulation or specific bank supervisory matters such as bank examination ratings or potential enforcement actions. Reserve Bank officials and directors told us that when supervision and regulation staff report on the operations in board meetings, they do not provide details on examination issues or identify institutions by name. Our review of board minutes showed a few instances where supervision and regulation staff shared summary information concerning the general condition of banking institutions in the district.

According to Federal Reserve Board and Reserve Bank officials, because the Federal Reserve Board has delegated the examination of bank and financial holding companies, member banks, and affiliates to the Reserve Bank staff, the staff report through the Reserve Bank presidents to the Federal Reserve Board and not directly to the boards of directors of the Reserve Bank. Further, although Supervision and Regulation generally reviews and approves member bank applications to purchase other banks or establish branch offices, among other things, applications that involve institutions affiliated with a Reserve Bank director are approved by the Federal Reserve Board. As an example, Goldman Sachs's application to become a bank holding company in September 2008 was reviewed by the Federal Reserve Board because one of the company's directors was also a director on the board of the Reserve Bank.

Questions also have been raised about the role of the Reserve Bank board in approving the Reserve Banks' discount window lending and whether conflicts of interest arise because officials from member banks that borrow from the discount window may serve as Class A directors on Reserve Bank boards. To avoid this potential conflict, no boards take part in loan approval, although some boards ratify loans that have already been granted under the discount window on a quarterly basis. Moreover, directors and Reserve Bank officials we spoke with said that Class A directors recuse themselves from the loan approval discussion when their institution has borrowed.

Conflict of Interest Policies

As explained more fully earlier, Reserve Bank directors are subject to the federal criminal conflict of interest restrictions under 18 U.S.C. § 208, which generally prohibits Reserve Bank directors from participating personally and substantially in their official capacities in any matter in which, to their knowledge, they have a financial interest, if the particular matter will have a direct and predictable effect on that interest. In addition, Reserve Bank directors are expected to follow relevant policies in the FRAM developed by the Federal Reserve Board. As stated in the FRAM's "Guide to Conduct for Directors of the Federal Reserve Banks and Branches," directors are expected to be "above reproach" in their personal financial dealings and should never use information they obtain as directors for personal gain. The FRAM states that in carrying out their responsibilities, directors should avoid any action that might result in or create the appearance of (1) affecting adversely the confidence of the public in the integrity of the Federal Reserve System, (2) using their position as director for private gain, or (3) giving unwarranted preferential treatment to any organization or person. Moreover, it states that directors should strictly preserve the confidentiality of Reserve Bank and Federal Reserve System information, and should avoid making public statements that suggest the nature of any monetary policy action that has not been officially disclosed. Directors also are expected to adhere to high ethical standards of conduct. In addition, directors are also expected to comply fully with all applicable laws and regulations governing their actions as directors and in their conduct outside of the Federal Reserve System.[45] The FRAM also prohibits directors from engaging in certain types of political activities. As a general principle, it states that directors should not engage in any political activity or serve in any public office where such activity or service might be interpreted as associating the Reserve Bank or the Federal Reserve System with any political party or partisan political activity, might embarrass the Reserve Bank or the Federal Reserve System in the conduct of its operations, or might raise any question as to the independence of the individual's judgment or ability to perform his or her duties with the Reserve Bank or System. The Federal Reserve Board's policy does not prohibit directors from participating in activities as individual voters or as members of nonpartisan public service bodies when that would not be potentially embarrassing to the Federal Reserve System.

Internal Controls

The Reserve Banks have internal controls, including annual certifications, oaths, and affirmations, to help the banks monitor directors' compliance with the FRAM and conflict of interest policies and procedures. These mechanisms require directors to report new directorships or affiliations, and to reaffirm that they are free of conflicts of interest. While directors are not required to disclose their financial holdings, Reserve Banks provide updates to directors whenever there is a change to the list of prohibited investments and affiliations (based on institutions that become bank holding companies or other institutions supervised by the Federal Reserve System). Also, during the directors' selection process, Reserve Bank officials conduct a background check using publicly available information on the directors and the financial status of the directors' companies. Once directors are on the board, the Reserve Banks rely on the directors to self report any actual or potential conflicts of interest. Additionally, the directors receive training at the beginning of their terms, from both the Reserve Bank and the Federal Reserve Board. The Federal Reserve Board training includes meetings where the directors are able to meet the Board of Governors, Federal Reserve Board staff, and other directors from across the system. The training provided by the Reserve Banks includes information on the FRAM's "Guide to Conduct for Directors of Federal Reserve Banks and Branches," roles and responsibilities, ethics, oaths, affidavits, and certifications. Many directors also receive ethics training annually, in addition to the beginning of their terms. Reserve Banks provide training to directors to guide them in determining what investments/affiliations may be prohibited. The Federal Reserve Board also offers midterm training to all directors, which officials said is generally well attended.

According to Federal Reserve Board and Reserve Bank officials with whom we spoke, the most likely potential conflict of interest involves procurement matters, and the Reserve Banks have taken a variety of steps to address them. Some Reserve Bank boards are involved in approving the bank's vendor contracts. Because some directors are affiliated with businesses in the banks' district that may offer services the Reserve Bank seeks, they could potentially have a conflict of interest if their firms or competitors were to compete for the contracts. To help ensure that procurement practices are untainted by actual or potential conflicts of interest from directors, the Federal

Reserve Board requires all of the Reserve Banks to have procurement policies that provide guidance for directors that includes the role of directors in procurements, the nature of the procurement, an education program for directors, written procedures for the directors to follow for recusal, written certification process, and record keeping of training materials and attendance, recusals, and procurement certifications. Our review noted that all banks require the directors to sign certifications stating whether or not they have a conflict of interest with a procurement that is being considered. All Reserve Banks have processes and certifications to help ensure that directors do not have conflicts. Likewise, all Reserve Banks have delegated certain procurement decisions to management.

Table 2. Comparison of Key Ethics Policies for Board Members at Selected Central Banks and the U.S. Federal Reserve Banks, as of July 2011

	Reserve Bank of Australia	Bank of Canada	Bank of England	European Central Bank	U.S. Federal Reserve Banks
Directors are required to					
Maintain confidentiality of information obtained through the board	Yes	Yes	Yes	Yes	Yes
Avoid even the appearance of a conflict of interest	Yes[a]	Yes	No[b]	Yes	Yes
Disclose conflicts of interest to the organization	Yes	Yes	Yes	Yes	No[c]
Not vote on issues for which they have a conflict	Yes[d]	Yes	Yes	No[e]	Yes
Annually disclose nonfinancial affiliations	Yes	Yes	Yes	Yes	No[f]
Annually disclose financial interests	Yes	No	No[g]	No[h]	No
Annually certify adherence to the ethics code	No	Yes[i]	No	No	No[j]

Source: GAO analysis of selected central bank authorizing legislation, ethics policies and procedures, and contact with central bank officials.

[a] Australia requires directors to avoid the appearance of using confidential information from the bank for personal profit. It does not require directors to avoid the appearance of

conflicts in general, just to promptly disclose them to the board. However, board members must consult with the governor before committing themselves to any material personal interest that might be perceived as creating a risk of conflict of interest.

[b] The Bank of England Act 1998 states that directors must disclose any direct and indirect interests in any dealing or business with the bank.

[c] The *Federal Reserve Administrative Manual* does not explicitly require directors to disclose conflicts of interest. Directors are required to adhere to a high ethical standard of conduct and avoid actions that might impair the effectiveness of system operations or in any way tend to discredit the system. Each Reserve Bank requires directors to sign certifications stating whether or not they have a conflict of interest with any procurement that is being considered. Directors at each Reserve Bank told us that they would report conflicts or changes in affiliations to a Reserve Bank official, such as the corporate secretary, general counsel, or ethics officer.

[d] Members of the Reserve Bank board, including the governor and deputy governor, are subject to a "Class order" of the treasurer, which waives conflicts of interest and allows them to participate in the board's monetary and financial stability policy deliberations, and decisions on indemnities to board members, subject to them providing the treasurer with an annual statement of material personal interests. For issues other than monetary policy and financial stability policy, and decisions on indemnities to board members, members must disclose conflicts of interest to the board, which will determine whether or not they are allowed to participate in discussion and consideration about such matters.

[e] The "Code of Conduct for the Governing Council" does not explicitly exclude voting in situations in case of a conflict of interests but stipulates that members of the Governing Council should avoid any situation liable to give rise to a conflict of interests and that they should be in a position to act with full independence and impartiality. However Executive Board members are prohibited from voting in cases in which they are personally affected by a prospective decision under certain articles.

[f] Directors do not submit an annual disclosure, but Class B and Class C directors submit an annual certification stating that they do not have any prohibited affiliations. Class C directors also submit a similar annual certification stating that they do not have any prohibited stockholdings. The directors are required to notify the corporate secretary if there are any changes in their affiliations or stockholdings, as appropriate.

[g] Only governors on the Court of Directors are required to report financial transactions.

[h] Only Executive Board members must file a financial disclosure, but there is no specific requirement regarding the frequency of such filing.

[i] The Bank of Canada does not have an ethics policy; directors have to certify compliance with its conflict-of-interest policy.

[j] Banks make an annual ethics presentation to their boards and get written certifications to adhere to the ethics code from new directors each year. Some banks do not get written certification from every director each year.

Federal Reserve Banks' Ethics Policies and Practices Are Generally Consistent with other Organizations' Policies and Practices, but Waiver Policies Could be Improved

We compared the Federal Reserve System's ethics and related policies and practices with those of other organizations, including other central banks, a self-regulatory organization whose members serve on its board of directors, a government-sponsored enterprise, and large bank holding companies. See appendix IV for a list of the 10 largest bank holding companies included in our review.

Written Ethics Policies for Reserve Banks and other Central Banks Reviewed Were Similar

The authorizing laws, policies, and procedures for all four central banks we studied, like the authorizing law, policies, and procedures for the Federal Reserve System, included provisions relating to ethical behavior and conduct. All four central banks and the U.S. Reserve Banks emphasized that directors must demonstrate a high level of ethical conduct and adhere to applicable laws and regulations, but policies for managing conflicts of interest varied. For example, the Reserve Bank of Australia waives all conflict of interest requirements for its board, and allows directors to participate in policy deliberations as long as they disclose their interests to the bank annually. However, the Reserve Bank of Australia prohibits directors from working for or having a material financial interest in private financial companies in Australia. Conversely, the Bank of Canada Act requires that directors (1) disclose any material interest in writing or in the minutes of board meetings, (2) disclose the conflict as quickly as possible after the conflict is discovered or realized, and (3) not vote in any resolution or action related to the conflict. Directors must also avoid or withdraw from participation in any activity or situation that places them in a real, potential, or apparent conflict of interest. The Bank of Canada prohibits directors from having affiliations with entities that perform clearing and settlement functions in the financial services industry, serving as a dealer for government securities, or being government employees. Table 2 provides additional information on the ethics and conflict-of-interest practices of the central banks we reviewed.

Federal Reserve Banks' Written Ethics Policies Are Generally Consistent with Those of Comparable Organizations

Reserve Banks' ethics policies were generally consistent with those of FINRA and those required of the FHLBanks and public companies listed on the New York Stock Exchange (NYSE). FINRA prohibits directors who have a substantial financial interest or are affiliated with a regulated entity from participating in any regulatory matter, disciplinary action, investigation, or decision regarding an application from that entity for an exemption. The Federal Housing Finance Agency—FHLBanks' regulator—requires that FHLBanks have a conflict of interest policy and that directors promptly disclose any actual or apparent conflicts of interest and recuse themselves from issues in which they have a conflict. Public companies listed on the NYSE—including the 10 largest bank holding companies included in our review—must adopt and disclose a code of business conduct and ethics. The code must contain a policy that prohibits conflicts of interest and allows directors to communicate potential conflicts with the company. Table 3 shows the ethics and conflict of interest practices of the comparable organizations we reviewed.

Federal Reserve Banks' Requirements for Directors to Disclose Affiliations Were Comparable to Those of other Organizations, but Waiver Policies Could be Improved

Federal Reserve Banks do not require directors to periodically disclose their financial interests. Officials at the Federal Reserve Board stated that directors were doing a civic duty by serving on a Reserve Bank board and that the Federal Reserve Board does not want to make it burdensome for them to serve. The officials also noted that directors' investments may change frequently, so keeping accurate information on all investments would be difficult. Class C directors submit an annual certification stating that they do not have any prohibited stockholdings. Although Federal Reserve Bank directors do not submit an annual disclosure of nonfinancial interests, both Class B and Class C directors are required to submit an annual certification stating that they do not have any prohibited affiliations. The directors are required to notify the corporate secretary if there are any changes in their affiliations or stockholdings, as appropriate. All four central banks we reviewed required directors to disclose some information about their personal

Table 3. Comparison of Key Ethics Policies for FINRA, FHLBanks, Large Bank Holding Companies, and the U.S. Federal Reserve Banks, as of July 2011

	Financial Industry Regulatory Authority	Federal Home Loan Banks	Large bank holding companies	U.S. Federal Reserve Banks
Directors are required to				
Maintain confidentiality of information obtained through the board	Yes	Yes	Yes	Yes
Avoid even the appearance of a conflict of interest	Yes	Yes	Yes	Yes
Disclose conflicts of interest to the organization	Yes	Yes	Yes	No[a]
Not vote on issues for which they have a conflict	Yes	Yes	Yes	Yes
Annually disclose non-financial affiliations	Yes	Yes[b]	Yes[b]	No[c]
Annually disclose financial interests	Yes[d]	No[e]	No NYSE listing requirement	No
Annually certify adherence to the ethics code	Yes	Yes[e]	3 out of 10	No[f]

Source: GAO analysis of FINRA, FHLBank, and FRB ethics policies and NYSE listing standards, and contact with agency officials.

[a] The *Federal Reserve Administrative Manual* does not explicitly require directors to disclose conflicts of interest. Directors are required to adhere to a high ethical standard of conduct and avoid actions that might impair the effectiveness of system operations or in any way tend to discredit the system. Each Reserve Bank requires directors to sign certifications stating whether or not they have a conflict of interest with any procurement that is being considered. Directors at each Reserve Bank told us that they would report conflicts or changes in affiliations to a Reserve Bank official, such as the corporate secretary, general counsel, or ethics officer.

[b] FHLBanks and other issuers of securities registered with the Securities and Exchange Commission, such as most large bank holding companies, are required to file an annual report that includes, among other things, information on the directorships held by each director during the last 5 years at any other public company or investment company.

[c] Directors do not submit an annual disclosure, but Class B and Class C directors submit an annual certification stating that they do not have any prohibited affiliations. Class C directors also submit a similar annual certification stating that they do not have any prohibited stockholdings. The directors are required to notify the corporate secretary if there are any changes in their affiliations or stockholdings, as appropriate.

[d] FINRA requires disclosure of board members' or his/her firm's financial interest in any covered entity—defined as any self-regulatory organization, broker-dealer, insurance company, investment company, investment adviser, or an affiliate of any such entity.

[e] Indicates what most FHLBanks reported as their practice.

[f] Banks make an annual ethics presentation to their boards and get written certifications to adhere to the ethics code from new directors each year. Some banks do not get written certification from every director each year.

affiliations with other organizations, such as other directorships. The Reserve Bank of Australia requires directors to disclose material personal financial interests—including financial and nonfinancial—to the treasurer on a yearly basis. The European Central Bank (ECB) requires all Governing Council members (i.e., Executive Board members and governors of the National Central Banks) to annually disclose their public and private affiliations, and Executive Board members must also complete a yearly financial disclosure.

FINRA governors annually disclose their relationships with other organizations, such as other directorships, but do not typically provide financial information annually, according to FINRA officials. FHLBanks are required to file an annual report on Form 10-K with the Securities and Exchange Commission. This form includes information about the directors' other directorships on the boards of publicly traded companies or investment companies. Most FHLBanks do not require directors to file a comprehensive annual financial disclosure, but most of the banks require directors to sign an annual certification agreeing to adhere to the ethics policies. All public companies—including the bank holding companies we reviewed—are also required by SEC to file a Form 10-K, which includes information about any other directorships of board members.

Other comparable organizations had a variety of policies on waiving ethics and related requirements. Central banks in our review varied in the extent to which they had policies or procedures for directors to apply for waivers to their ethics policies. The Bank of Canada does not have a waiver process. An official at the bank stated that waivers would be inconsistent with the bank's conflict of interest policy, which requires that directors avoid or withdraw from participation in any activity that places the director in a real, potential, or apparent conflict of interest. The European Central Bank Code of Conduct instructs Governing Council members to seek counsel from an ethics adviser if a conflict arises. The adviser either decides the issue or forwards it to the Governing Council. The NYSE requires that listed companies, including the large bank holding companies we reviewed, promptly disclose any waivers of codes of conduct for directors or executive directors. Only boards and board committees can grant waivers, which must be disclosed to shareholders within 4 business days, using either a press release, the institutional website, or an SEC Form 8-K. FINRA's code of conduct for directors states the board must approve waivers from the code. However, FINRA officials told us that in practice, its governors have chosen to manage conflicts through recusal rather than seeking waivers. About half of the FHLBanks reported that they have a process in place for directors to request a waiver of the code of conduct.

There are two types of waivers relevant to Reserve Bank directors. First, as discussed earlier, the Federal Reserve Board can grant waivers to directors in connection with 18 U.S.C. §208, pursuant to applicable federal regulations. Second, Reserve Banks may request waivers from the Federal Reserve Board's policies related to director eligibility, qualifications and rotation, such as allowing directors to remain on the Reserve Bank board despite having a prohibited investment or other prohibited affiliation. Federal Reserve Board officials said they have received few waiver requests. According to the officials, the Federal Reserve Board waiver process permits Reserve Banks to make informal inquiries of Federal Reserve Board staff as to whether a given action would be appropriate. The officials noted that most of the time Reserve Banks' questions could be resolved without an official waiver request. Additionally, Reserve Bank officials told us that they frequently receive questions from directors about the policies, which they either discuss and handle internally, or contact the ethics officer or corporate secretary at the Federal Reserve Board to determine the appropriate actions that should be taken. For example, one director checked with the general counsel at the Reserve Bank to discuss a situation in which family members had inherited bank stock that was held in a trust for which the director was named trustee. The general counsel discussed the issue with relevant officials at the Reserve Bank and advised the director to resign his position in the trust so that he would not have a conflict of interest.

Not all Reserve Banks have procedures in place for directors to request a waiver of the eligibility policy from the Federal Reserve Board. We found that the Reserve Banks are not required to have a waiver request process and only

FRBNY has a formal process in place to review waiver requests. An official from one Reserve Bank told us that the bank does not have a formal process for considering waiver requests nor has it had directors who needed to request a waiver from the Federal Reserve Board. When FRBNY sought the waiver on behalf of the then-FRBNY chairman from the Federal Reserve Board, FRBNY did not have a formal waiver process and did not consult with the board of directors before making a waiver request to the Federal Reserve Board. An FRBNY official told us that in hindsight the board should have been involved. On the basis of this experience, FRBNY implemented a formal waiver process. While we recognize that the need to request a waiver from Federal Reserve Board policies may be rare, a crisis situation may create unanticipated conflicts without providing time for comprehensive actions before a decision must be made. However, without a formal process in place to consider a request for a waiver from Federal Reserve Board policies, Reserve Banks risk inconsistent treatment of requests and being exposed to questions about their governance practice and the integrity of their decisions and actions.[46]

If waivers to policies are granted, making the process and decisions transparent is vital. Given the public nature of Reserve Bank activities, disclosing waivers provided to directors is one way to improve transparency and accountability and reduce the appearance of conflicts of interest. Public companies listed on the NYSE are required to promptly disclose any waivers of the code of conduct for directors and executive officers, which can be made only by the board or a committee of the board. To the extent that a waiver of the code of conduct is granted, the waiver must be disclosed to shareholders within 4 business days of the decision, by distributing a press release, providing website disclosure, or filing a report with SEC. Reserve Banks are not required to disclose information to the public about waivers of the policy on director eligibility and qualifications for one of their directors that were granted by the Federal Reserve Board. As demonstrated during the recent financial crisis and the waiver request for the then-FRBNY chairman, a lack of transparency around the waiver request process and outcome contributed to greater distrust of Reserve Bank governance.

Additional Steps Are Needed to Improve Transparency and Accountability

Congress and the Federal Reserve System have taken steps aimed at improving Reserve Bank governance. The Dodd-Frank Act, enacted on July

21, 2010, made several amendments to the Federal Reserve Act. One of these amendments changed the selection process for Reserve Bank presidents and first vice presidents. Before the amendment, all directors acted to appoint the president of the Reserve Bank, subject to the approval of the Federal Reserve Board.[47] This created the appearance of a conflict because the Class A directors voted to appoint the Reserve Bank president, who would play a role in supervision and regulation and may be a voting member of the FOMC.[48] After the amendment, only Class B directors (who are elected by district member banks to represent the public) and Class C directors (who are appointed by the Federal Reserve Board to represent the public) may appoint the Reserve Bank presidents. Class A directors, who are elected by member banks to represent member banks, may no longer appoint presidents of the Federal Reserve Banks. This same change also affects the appointment of the first vice president.

In part because of the financial crisis that started in mid 2007 and the increased scrutiny of the Federal Reserve System, the Federal Reserve Board conducted a study of the governance of the Federal Reserve Banks, which included a review of the roles and responsibilities of the Reserve Bank directors. In November 2009, the results of this study were presented to the Reserve Bank presidents, corporate secretaries, and board chairmen, which led some banks to conduct reviews of the roles and responsibilities of their bank directors. As a result of the Federal Reserve Board review, the board revised two policies governing directors.

First, the board amended the eligibility policy to explicitly address situations in which Class B or C directors' stockholdings unexpectedly become impermissible, such as if a company in which a director holds stock converts to a bank holding company. Before this revision, the Federal Reserve Board did not have a formal policy governing the treatment of such situations. The revised policy requires directors to resign from the board or divest their interests within 60 days from the time the Reserve Bank or director learned about an impermissible situation. During this time, the director would have to recuse himself or herself from all duties related to service as a Reserve Bank director until the affiliation is severed. Second, the Federal Reserve Board revised its policy on director conduct by requiring Reserve Banks to adopt a policy that governs instances when directors are involved with procurement, as discussed previously.

Since this Federal Reserve Board study and the Dodd-Frank Act amendments, all of the Reserve Banks have changed the directors' roles to remove the Class A directors from the process of appointing the bank president. In addition, some banks have included additional restrictions on Class A directors' involvement in supervision and regulation personnel and other matters. For example, the Federal Reserve Banks of New York, Richmond, and Minneapolis restricted Class A directors' involvement in personnel appointments for supervision and regulation. Moreover, after the recent study, the board of the Federal Reserve Bank of St. Louis reevaluated its procedures so that the Class A directors are not involved with personnel matters related to the senior vice president of its supervision and regulation function, or any institution-specific matters.

According to Federal Reserve System officials, it has been a standing practice, predating the enactment of the Dodd-Frank Act, that Reserve Bank directors do not vote on institution-specific supervisory matters. Beyond that practice, the Federal Reserve Banks of New York, Richmond, St. Louis, and Minneapolis recently revised their bylaws to include the role of their boards of directors with regard to supervision and regulation. FRBNY made clear that Class A directors are prohibited from voting on appointment, termination, and compensation of employees in the Financial Institutions Supervision group. Federal Reserve Bank of Richmond stated directors cannot vote on institution-specific supervision and regulation matters and that Class A directors should not vote on the budget for the supervision and regulation function and matters related to senior personnel in that function. Federal Reserve Bank of St. Louis states that actions by the board of directors related to oversight of the supervision and regulation function shall be upon a vote of a majority of the Class B and Class C directors present at any such meeting. Similarly, Federal Reserve Bank of Minneapolis stated that directors are not involved in institution-specific supervision and regulation matters and Class A and Class B directors should not vote on matters of an administrative nature.

Although there are restrictions on directors' involvement in supervision and regulation matters, the Reserve Banks are not required to document the directors' roles in their bylaws. As a result, 8 of the 12 Reserve Banks have not documented the extent of board of directors' involvement in supervision and regulation in their bylaws. The Federal Reserve Banks of Boston, Chicago, Cleveland, Dallas, Kansas City, Philadelphia, and San Francisco do not document the directors' roles and responsibilities to further clarify the extent of their involvement in supervision and regulation matters.

Although Reserve Bank directors may be cognizant of their roles and responsibilities, a lack of a clear statement in the bylaws on the directors' involvement in supervision and regulation matters could contribute to lack of clarity around the directors' roles, create confusion for the public, and lead to questions about Reserve Bank governance. Moreover, by documenting the roles of directors with regard to such matters, the Federal Reserve System could help enhance the public's understanding of the roles of the directors and reduce the appearance of conflicts of interest.

Changes to the Structure of the Reserve Banks' Boards to Further Strengthen Governance Involve Trade-Offs

Some officials, directors, and academics with whom we spoke also suggested potential changes to the Reserve Bank board structure that could further strengthen governance, but these changes would involve tradeoffs. First, some suggested that increasing the number of directors appointed by the Federal Reserve Board who represent the public could help alleviate the appearance of member bank control. This could be accomplished by expanding the Reserve Bank board size by increasing the number of Class C directors or by adding a fourth class of 3 directors appointed by the Federal Reserve Board. By adding 3 more appointed directors to the Reserve Bank board, the boards would have an equal number of directors elected by member banks and directors appointed by the Federal Reserve Board, therefore eliminating the perception of member bank control of the boards. We have previously reported that board size is not one-size-fits-all and should be based on the needs and complexity of the organization.[49] As discussed later in the report, board size for other public and private organizations varies, but a board size of 12 members would still be within the range of board sizes at other comparable organizations such as central banks, self-regulatory organizations, and large bank holding companies. A larger board could also enhance opportunities for diverse candidates. However, adding 3 board members would create more positions for Reserve Banks to fill, and it may be more difficult for some of the Reserve Banks to fill these positions. As of September 16, 2011, there were two director positions in the 12 Reserve Banks open. Additionally, some Reserve Bank officials and directors stated that a larger board size could reduce the opportunity for directors to participate in the meeting and may increase absences or decrease committee participation because directors could feel that their contributions were less important because there were more directors to accomplish the necessary board work. Additionally, an increase in the size of the Reserve Bank board would require an amendment to the Federal Reserve Act.

Second, some Reserve Bank officials and directors suggested that the Federal Reserve Board could appoint Class B directors to represent the public rather than having them elected by member banks. The perception of conflicts of interest and member bank control could be reduced by making this change. However, we heard from several academics and Reserve Bank officials that the current system provides a set of checks and balances between the Federal Reserve Board in Washington, D.C., and the 12 Reserve Banks and their members. By allowing the Federal Reserve Board to appoint two-thirds of the Reserve Bank boards, the balance of power would shift to the Federal Reserve Board. Officials and directors we spoke with emphasized the importance of regional input in the Federal Reserve System, which includes the ability of the regions to select their representatives on the Reserve Bank board. Additionally, as discussed earlier, while the FRAM prohibits bank officials and employees from serving on nomination committees for Class A and B directors, Reserve Bank officials told us that they played a significant role in the identification, vetting, and recruiting of Class B directors before they are nominated and elected by member banks. Because Reserve Bank officials are involved in the identification and vetting process for both types of candidates, whether changing the selection process for Class B directors would change the outcome significantly is unclear. Additionally, allowing the Federal Reserve Board to appoint the Class B directors would require an amendment to the Federal Reserve Act.

Changes to the Federal Reserve System Structure Also Involve Trade-Offs

Congress, academics, and others have offered a number of ways to change the structure of the Federal Reserve System, which would have implications for governance and ongoing concerns about conflicts of interest. First, some academics and others have commented that the Reserve Banks should become offices or branches of the Federal Reserve Board rather than independent entities within the system, which would eliminate the boards of directors, or they said the boards of directors should be converted into advisory councils. One academic told us that making them branches would help address concerns about the current governance structure because it would eliminate the need for boards of directors and thereby eliminate conflicts. As an example, the central bank of Germany follows this model. However, others we interviewed noted that this would concentrate all of the power and influence with the Federal

Reserve Board. Moreover, it would increase the size of the federal agency. In addition, others have said that converting boards to advisory councils in the districts would undermine governance by reducing the responsibility of the boards and would make it harder to attract quality candidates to serve on the councils.

Second, some have questioned the need for 12 Reserve Banks given changes in the financial markets and advances in technology. The views of Federal Reserve System officials varied. A few of the individuals we interviewed thought there could be fewer banks because the current structure was outdated and reflected a U.S. economy that existed 100 years ago. However, others believe that the structure is still appropriate given differences in regional economies and perspectives. Federal Reserve System officials also point to the greater efficiencies that have been implemented through the Reserve Banks' consolidation of certain ongoing operations such as check clearing and information technology.

Third, some in Congress and others recommended that the Federal Reserve System's role in supervision and regulation be eliminated, which would have eliminated concerns about conflicts of interest involving directors affiliated with institutions supervised by the Reserve Banks. Some believe that the central bank should be focused exclusively on monetary policy and that supervision and regulation should be conducted by another regulatory entity. Others viewed the two functions as critically intertwined, and ultimately, this approach to reform was not pursued by Congress in the Dodd-Frank Act. Rather, the Federal Reserve System's supervisory role was increased to include thrift holding companies and systemically important financial institutions. Others have taken a less sweeping approach to reform by questioning the Federal Reserve Board's delegation of supervision to the Reserve Banks. However, consolidating supervision with the Federal Reserve Board would require a substantial increase in the federal workforce for the Federal Reserve Board to conduct this function. Currently, the supervision and regulation staff at the Reserve Banks are not federal employees because they are employees of the Reserve Banks and not the Federal Reserve Board. Rather, the Reserve Bank supervision and regulation staff act under authority delegated from and are overseen by the Federal Reserve Board. With the exception of the delegation of authority, these other structural changes involve policy decisions that would require changes to the Federal Reserve Act.

ALTHOUGH MOST FEDERAL RESERVE BANKS' GOVERNANCE PRACTICES ARE CONSISTENT WITH THOSE OF OTHER ORGANIZATIONS, BOARD GOVERNANCE COULD BE MORE TRANSPARENT

Reserve Bank boards are generally similar in size, composition, and term lengths and limits to the boards of comparable organizations. Additionally, they employ similar accountability measures, such as annual performance reviews of the organization and management, as other comparable organizations. However, Reserve Banks lack transparency in their governance practices compared with those of other organizations we reviewed. For example, while most all of the other organizations we reviewed make key governance documents, such as board bylaws, ethics policies, committee mission statements, and committee assignments, available to the public, most Reserve Banks do not post this information on their websites.

Reserve Banks' Board Structure and Independence Requirements Are Similar to Those of Comparable Organizations

As previously discussed, the size of Reserve Bank boards is established by the Federal Reserve Act of 1913 and sets each board's size at nine directors. The size of the Reserve Bank boards is within the range of board sizes and composition that we identified at comparable organizations. As we have seen, the boards of the organizations we studied had from 9 to 23 members (see table 4). Neither the NYSE nor SEC has size requirements for the boards of listed and public companies, and most of the bank holding companies we reviewed included provisions in their bylaws that allowed for flexibility in board size. For example, one company's bylaws state the board has the authority to determine the number of directors and that the number should be in the range of 13 to 19, with the flexibility to increase the size as needs and circumstances change. The number of allowable directors under the bylaws of bank holding companies we studied ranged from 3 to 36, while the actual number of directors on the boards of bank holding companies included in our study ranged from 11 to 15.

Table 4. Size and Composition of Boards of Directors of Federal Reserve Banks Compared with Those of Selected Entities, as of August 2011

Characteristics	Reserve Bank of Australia	Bank of Canada	Bank of England	European Central Bank	Financial Industry Regulatory Authority	Federal Home Loan Banks	Federal Reserve Bank
Size of board	9	15	12	23	22[a]	13-18[b]	9
Number of board members who are independent[c]	5-6[d]	12	9	0[e]	11	At least 2/5 of board	6[f]
Number of board members representing member institutions	Not applicable	Not applicable	Not applicable	17	10[g]	No more than 3/5	3[h]
Number of board members employed by the institution or government	3-4	3[i]	3	6	1	0	0

Source: GAO analysis of selected central bank authorizing legislation, and FINRA and FHLB bylaws and websites reviewed between March 8, 2011 and August 24, 2011.

[a] FINRA bylaws provide that the board shall consist of between 16 and 25 governors; the number of public governors must exceed the number of industry governors.

[b] Section 7(a) of the Federal Home Loan Bank Act, as amended, generally sets the size of a Bank's board of directors at 13, but the size of each FHLB board can vary because of another statutory provision.

[c] "Independent" means not affiliated with the organization, the government, or a member institution.

[d] One of the six "other" board members can be an official (Reserve Bank of Australia [RBA] or Australian government) who holds office at the pleasure of the treasurer. Therefore, there could be 5- 6 board members who are unaffiliated with the RBA and 3-4 board members who work for the RBA or Australian government.

[e] The European Central Bank's Governing Council includes the governors of the national central banks of the 17 euro area countries.

[f] Federal Reserve Banks have six directors who represent the public. Three of these directors (Class B) are elected by member banks, but cannot be officers, directors, or employees at any bank. The other three directors (Class C) are appointed by the Federal Reserve Board and also cannot be officers, directors, shareholders, or employees at any bank.

[g] Three of these governors are not required to be from institutions that are members of FINRA, but they are required to be affiliated with one of the following industry groups (1) a floor broker, (2) an independent broker-dealer or insurance company, or (3) a registered investment company.

[h] These three directors (Class A) are not required to be officers or directors of member banks, but they generally are.

[i] The Deputy Minister of Finance is a member of the board but does not have the right to vote.

According to NYSE, independence for directors means having no material relationship with the listed company, either directly or as a partner, shareholder, or officer of an organization that has a relationship with the company. Central bank literature typically refers to independence in terms of the central bank being independent of the government; therefore, independent directors are those who do not work for the central bank or other government entity. Independence is an important aspect of board governance because it provides accountability and an outside perspective. Further, the Organisation for Economic Co-operation and Development (OECD) notes that boards must be able to exercise objective judgment in order to fulfill their duties and that, to accomplish this goal, a sufficient number of board members should be independent of management.[50]

Reserve Bank directors have varying levels of independence. As discussed earlier in this report, Class C directors are appointed by the Federal Reserve Board. These directors are independent—that is, they are not employees or managers of the Reserve Banks at which they serve, nor are they a partner, shareholder, or officer of an organization that has a relationship with the Reserve Bank, such as a member bank. Class B directors are elected by member banks and are statutorily required to represent the public. They meet almost all of the independence requirements listed above, with the exception that they can be a stockholder in a bank. Class A directors, who represent the member banks that elect them, are the least independent of the Reserve Bank directors. Some have questioned whether Reserve Bank boards have enough independence from the member banks that the Reserve Banks supervise. FINRA's bylaws balance public and industry representation by requiring that members representing the public outnumber those representing industry on the board. No FHLBank managers serve on the FHLBank boards, and by law at least two-fifths of the directors must be independent and not affiliated with member banks.[51] Additionally, at least two of the independent directors must be "public interest" directors with at least 4 years of experience representing community or consumer interests in banking services, credit needs, housing, or consumer financial protections.

Term Lengths and Limits and Selection Procedures Were Comparable across Organizations

Reserve Bank directors' term lengths and limits were also within the range of term lengths and limits we observed for other comparable entities. For example, both Reserve Bank and FINRA directors can serve up to two consecutive 3-year terms. At the other four central banks we reviewed, independent directors—who are not government or central bank officials, or for the ECB, the board members from national central banks—served 3- to 5-year terms. Other board members (including governors and other government officials) served 5- to 8-year terms. FHLB directors may serve up to three consecutive 4-year terms. The NYSE and SEC do not have requirements for listed or public companies regarding term length or limits. Two of the large bank holding companies we reviewed opted to have directors serve 1-year terms so that each director had to be reelected by the stockholders each year, but none of the companies enacted term limits for their directors. One company noted in its annual proxy statement that although term limits might be a source of fresh ideas and viewpoints, they had the disadvantage of potentially reducing the knowledge and insight that experienced directors gained over time. Another bank holding company's proxy statement said that the company favored monitoring individual director performance over term limits.

Selection procedures for directors varied across the entities we examined. As we have discussed, Federal Reserve Bank boards consist of both appointed and elected directors. However, all the boards of the four central banks we reviewed had directors who were appointed to the board by various entities. For example, for the ECB Executive Board, members are nominated by the governments of euro-area member states. Both the ECB's Governing Council and the European Parliament are consulted on prospective candidates and issue opinions on them. The European Parliament holds a hearing for the nominated candidate, and the European Council (only member states that have adopted the euro) votes to appoint a new Executive Board member. The 17 euro-area National Central Bank governors who are members of the Governing Council in addition to the 6 Executive Board members are selected according to national procedures. The directors of the Reserve Bank of Australia and independent directors of the Bank of Canada are appointed by the Treasurer and Minister of Finance, respectively. The Queen of England appoints governors and nonexecutive directors to the Court of Directors at the Bank of England.

The other comparable organizations we studied had a combination of elected and appointed members and used nominating committees as part of the director selection process. FINRA's bylaws require that all members be nominated by a committee and certified by the corporate secretary. Of the 10 industry directors, 7 are elected by their constituents. The 3 remaining industry directors and all of the public directors are appointed by FINRA's Board of Governors after nomination by the committee. FHLBank member directors are nominated and voted on by member institutions within their state, whereas independent directors are nominated by the FHLBank's board of directors, after consultation with its Advisory Council, and elected by the FHLBanks' members at-large. Companies listed on the NYSE must have nominating/corporate governance committees composed entirely of independent directors to identify qualified individuals and select them or recommend them to the board for selection. Stockholders elect the directors of the 10 largest bank holding companies we reviewed.

Like the Reserve Banks, other comparable entities also considered skills and experience as key factors in selecting board members. Reserve Banks recruit directors in accordance with the requirements in the Federal Reserve Act, which stipulate that directors shall be chosen without discrimination as to race, creed, color, sex, or national origin and that Class B and Class C directors who represent the public shall be elected "with due but not exclusive consideration to the interests of agriculture, commerce, industry, services, labor, and consumers." Some Reserve Bank officials told us that while they strive to find diverse candidates from a variety of industries, they primarily want to find people who have the skills and knowledge that will fill gaps in the board's existing knowledge and skill set. Similarly, all four central banks we reviewed had skill or experience qualifications for board members. For example, the Bank of Canada focuses on the collective skills of the board of directors in areas such as accounting, human resources, corporate governance, and financial markets.

FHLBanks and FINRA also look for directors with particular skills and experience to complement the boards. FHLBank nonmember directors are required to have experience in, or knowledge of, one or more of the following areas: auditing and accounting, derivatives, financial management, organizational management, project development, risk management practices, and the law. FINRA officials stated that they had no written qualifications but added that for each opening they analyzed the type of expertise the board lacked—for example, technological, legal, or academic—to identify skills that would complement the existing expertise. SEC requires public companies to disclose information about the qualifications of directors and nominees for director and to provide reasons why each should serve but does not require specific types of experience or expertise.

As with the Federal Reserve Banks, none of the comparable entities had specific requirements for gender or race and ethnic diversity for their boards. One central bank required that directors represent different geographies and industries within the country. As discussed earlier, public companies must report in their proxy and information statement on how the nominating committee considered diversity when reviewing candidates for director. In our analysis of the 10 largest bank holding companies in 2010, proxy statements indicated that companies primarily value candidates that will bring complementary skills and experience to the board but also consider diversity in selecting them.

Federal Reserve Banks' Accountability Measures Are Consistent with Comparable Organizations' Measures

Reserve Banks and comparable institutions, both public and private, have a variety of accountability measures in place, including annual performance reviews of the organization and management, internal and self-assessments, and external audits. All 12 Reserve Bank boards conduct bankwide performance reviews on a yearly basis. Similarly, a committee of the board at the Bank of England—the Committee of the Court (NedCo)—is responsible for reviewing the bank's performance in relation to its objectives and strategy, monitoring the extent to which its financial management objectives are met, reviewing the procedures of the Monetary Policy Committee and the bank's internal controls, and determining the pay and terms of employment of the governors, executive directors and external Monetary Policy Committee members. To a large extent, NedCo's work is done through the Court of Directors; it is chaired by the Court's chairman and consists of all nonexecutive members.

Internal reviews and self-assessments are also part of board accountability practices across the institutions that we reviewed. Within the Federal Reserve

System, the Federal Reserve Board relies on RBOPS to oversee Reserve Banks' management and operations. RBOPS reviews each Reserve Bank at least every 3 years. In addition, 6 of the 12 Federal Reserve Bank boards of directors conduct an annual self-evaluation. Some of the other organizations that we reviewed had similar evaluations conducted by their boards. For example, the Bank of similar evaluations conducted by their boards. For example, the Bank of Canada's board conducts an annual self-assessment through one-on-one interviews between each director and the lead director, supported by a survey that solicits directors' views on various elements of the board's operations, governance, and effectiveness. The survey is completed electronically and aggregated results are distributed to directors for discussion in open session. The board also has developed and maintains a skills map of the current directors' competencies and takes note of any gaps or deficiencies. Further, companies listed on the NYSE must adopt corporate governance guidelines that include provisions for the board to conduct a self-evaluation at least annually to determine whether it and its committees are functioning effectively.

Reserve Bank boards and publicly listed companies also hold meetings of nonmanagement directors to promote accountability by encouraging nonmanagement directors to serve as a more effective check on management. All Federal Reserve Bank boards have executive committees that vary across banks in terms of the composition of Class A, B, and C directors (see app. III for more information on the Reserve Bank committees). The NYSE requires that nonmanagement directors of each listed company meet at regularly scheduled executive sessions without management.

Some of the organizations that we reviewed, including the Federal Reserve Banks, had audit committees in place. Each Reserve Bank has an audit committee that oversees the bank's internal auditor and reviews and approves the annual audit plan. The audit committee is also responsible for coordinating with external auditors and helping ensure that audit recommendations and concerns are properly addressed. Similarly, the Bank of England has two committees that play a role in accountability. First, as previously discussed, the Committee of the Court, NedCo, is responsible for conducting a performance assessment of the central bank. Second, the Risk and Audit Committee provides independent assurance to the Court of Directors that the bank's internal controls are appropriate. The committee meets regularly and reviews the work of internal and external auditors, annual financial statements, and the appropriateness of the accounting policies and procedures adopted. It also makes recommendations on the appointment of the external auditors, including their independence and fees, and reviews the bank's risk matrix and specific business controls. The Reserve Bank of Australia and the Bank of Canada also have audit committees that play a role similar to that of the Reserve Banks' committees.

FINRA's bylaws require the board to have an audit committee of four or five governors, none of them officers or employees of the corporation and including at least two public governors. The audit committee's functions are similar to those of committees at other organizations previously discussed. Finally, NYSE-listed companies are required to have audit committees with at least three independent members. NYSE guidelines stipulate that audit committees must assist with board oversight of the company's financial statements, compliance with legal and regulatory requirements, the independent auditor's qualifications and independence, and the performance of the company's internal audit function and independent auditors. The audit committees are also responsible for SEC's required disclosures on committee activity.[52]

Although Reserve Banks Have Taken Steps to Make Their Governance Practices More Transparent, More Needs to Be Done

Governance practices should be transparent to protect organizational reputation and help ensure accountability. Reserve Bank governance practices lack transparency compared with those of comparable institutions that we reviewed. We have previously reported that good governance, transparency, and accountability are critical in both the private and public sectors.[53] In the private sector, they promote efficiency and effectiveness in the capital and credit markets, and overall economic growth, both domestically and internationally. In the public sector, they are essential to the effective and credible functioning of a healthy democracy and to fulfilling the government's responsibility to citizens and taxpayers. Additionally, the World Bank, the International Monetary Fund, OECD, and other researchers agree that transparency is an important principle in good governance.[54] While the Federal Reserve System has begun to increase the disclosure of information, more can be done to enhance the transparency of the Reserve Banks' governance practices.

Most Federal Reserve Banks Do Not Disclose Significant Information about Governance

Most Reserve Banks do not routinely disclose governance practices to the public, while most comparable institutions we reviewed do. For example, all four central banks we studied had public websites that displayed information about board governance, including information about the committee structure and conflict of interest policies. FINRA bylaws, including committee mission statements and conflict-of-interest rules, are also available on the FINRA website. The Federal Housing Finance Agency does not have any reporting requirements for FHLBanks, and while FHLBanks vary in what they publish on their websites, most provide some information. For example, three-quarters of the FHLBanks post information about their code of ethics, bylaws, or both, and half provide information about the election process, including time frames and independent director applications. One-third of the FHLBanks post biographical information about the directors beyond the director's company, position, and location. 6 of the 12 FHLBanks post information about the board committees—either a description of each committee and its purpose or board members serving on each committee, and six FHLBanks publish the audit committee charter on their websites.

Publicly traded companies were subject to the most stringent disclosure guidelines of the institutions we examined. The NYSE requires that listed companies publicly disclose corporate governance guidelines that address director qualification standards, responsibilities, compensation, and access to management and independent advisers, as well as director orientation and continuing education, management succession, and annual performance evaluations of the board. Corporate websites must be accessible from the United States, must clearly indicate in the English language the location of governance documents, and documents must be available in printable versions in English.

By comparison, few of the Reserve Banks post information about board governance, such as committee structure and assignments, or conflict of interest and ethics policies on their websites. While the Federal Reserve Board notes vacant positions among its list of Reserve Bank board directors, the Reserve Banks do not publish information about vacant director positions on their websites. Additionally, all Reserve Banks have publicly accessible websites, but most banks post only the names, titles, and employers of current directors rather than richer biographical information. Four of the Reserve Banks provide descriptions of the board and their roles, and two banks post more comprehensive information. For example, FRBNY includes the board's bylaws, biographies for current board members, the members and charters of each of the board's committees, and the bank president's daily schedule. Federal Reserve Bank of Kansas City posts information about the directors' selection and roles, biographies for current directors, and lists alumni directors from 1992 to the present.

A few individuals we spoke with noted that, in particular, Reserve Banks could be more transparent about director elections. One researcher stated that as a result of the lack of transparency around the director election process, there is a lack of understanding of how and why directors were chosen to serve on Reserve Bank boards. This can also cause increased concern about potential conflicts of interest among the directors because how and why certain individuals were selected for the board is not clear to the public. Further, in our survey of Reserve Bank directors, one director noted that transparency around the election process should be improved. The director noted that the topic was not discussed in board meetings or executive sessions of board meetings. Federal Reserve Board officials said that two Reserve Banks are publicly announcing board vacancies, but because Class A and B directors are elected by the member banks, Class C directors were the only vacancies for which the general public could apply. Further, officials said that while they could enhance transparency by advertising a vacant Class C position, the nature of the job and the need for a specific skill set generally meant that it was better for the banks themselves to recruit candidates instead of publicly seeking applications.

Enhanced transparency of the director selection process, including posting director vacancies and selection procedures, could not only make the election process more transparent but also help increase the diversity of the candidate pool. Some of the institutions we reviewed have taken steps to increase transparency of their director selection process. Two of the central banks we reviewed publicized and solicited applications for governor/director positions. It was announced in July 2008 that the Bank of England would advertise vacant positions. Additionally, in Canada, a government website permits individuals to submit their names for consideration as directors of government. Also ministers responsible for entities requiring directors maintain a pool of all eligible candidates, so the Minister of Finance develops this pool of candidates for the Bank of Canada. As previously noted, about half of the FHLBanks publish information on their websites about the director election process and provide applications for potential candidates to submit to be considered by the nomination committee. Further, as previously mentioned, some Members of

Congress and others raised questions about the governance of the Reserve Banks, including the selection and roles of directors. Improving the transparency of the Reserve Bank director selection process is one way to help address concerns about Reserve Bank governance.

The Federal Reserve System Can Take Additional Steps to Increase Transparency

The Federal Reserve System has taken some important steps to increase transparency. For example, the Federal Reserve Board has recently taken steps to increase transparency of the monetary policy-making process. In March, the Federal Reserve Board announced that the Chairman would hold press briefings four times per year to present the Federal Open Market Committee's current economic projections and to provide additional context for its policy decisions. The first press conference was held in April 2011. Additionally, some Reserve Banks have begun placing additional information about governance arrangements on their public websites. The Federal Reserve Board describes these postings as a recent trend and said that FRBNY has been a leader in this area.

Further, the Reserve Bank boards conduct community outreach that focuses primarily on financial literacy and informing the public on their role in monetary policy. One of the three main roles for Reserve Bank directors is to be a liaison between the bank and the community. Several directors and bank officials told us that they believe that public outreach was necessary to help reduce the public's misperception about the roles and responsibilities of the Reserve Banks. In our survey of Reserve Bank directors, some directors noted that outreach should be continued to create a more transparent environment and strengthen governance. For example, one director said that one way to strengthen Reserve Bank governance was to continue to foster an environment of transparency, with open and frequent communication. Further, the director noted that not everyone understood the difference between monetary and fiscal policy and that the Reserve Banks could help to educate the general public and the media. One director also noted that outreach activities generated goodwill and awareness throughout the community and the district and led to better public representation on Reserve Bank boards. Additionally, another director noted that the Reserve Banks needed to continue their outreach to educate the public about monetary policy and the need for an independent Federal Reserve System but cited the Reserve Banks' budget constraints as a limitation to their outreach efforts.

Officials at the Federal Reserve Board noted that the Federal Reserve System functions more effectively and efficiently when each Reserve Bank is implementing good governance procedures because good corporate governance is a key element in improving economic efficiency. Additionally, in a time when the relationships between directors and financial firms are being questioned, transparent governance practices can help in managing reputational risk. Moreover, when there is increased public interest in governance, the Federal Reserve System would be well served by making clear the roles and responsibilities of Reserve Bank directors. Moreover, without more public disclosure of governance arrangements, such as board bylaws and conflict-of-interest policies, there will be continued concerns about Reserve Bank governance.

CONCLUSION

The Federal Reserve System was designed as a decentralized entity with a governmental institution and 12 separately incorporated Reserve Banks. Under this public-private partnership, the Reserve Bank directors serve a role in bringing information from their communities to inform the monetary policy deliberations of the central bank and helping oversee the operations of the Reserve Banks. The directors, like the Federal Reserve Board, are also part of the governance framework of the Reserve Banks. However, the operations and governance of the Federal Reserve System came to the forefront during the 2007-2009 financial crisis when it played a prominent role in stabilizing financial markets through the use of its emergency lending authorities. These unprecedented actions resulted in Congress and the public raising questions about the Reserve Banks' governance practices and potential conflicts of interest involving the directors.

Specifically, some questioned how well the Reserve Bank boards represent the public, which in part could be measured by the economic and demographic diversity of the directors. Our analysis shows that from 2006 through 2010 labor and consumer groups tended to be less represented than other industry groups on both head office and branch boards. While the Federal Reserve Board encouraged the Reserve Banks to recruit directors from consumer and labor organizations, restrictions on directors' political activities appeared to be a challenge in recruiting representatives from these organizations, who tend to be politically active. Our analysis also shows that while there is some variation among the Reserve Banks in the representation of women and minorities at head office and branch boards, overall, it has remained limited. Although it is difficult to know whether the board's decisions would have been different had there been greater diversity on the boards, the public that the board represents is becoming increasingly diverse. Officials from most Reserve Banks generally focus their search for candidates on senior corporate executives, who are perceived to have a relatively broad perspective on the economy. However, seeking directors from among senior or chief-level executives may contribute to the limited diversity on the boards because as our analysis of EEOC data shows, diversity at the senior executive level is more limited than at the senior manager level across industries. To the extent that director searches are limited to chief-level executives, the Reserve Banks not only limit the diversity of the pool of potential candidates but also risk limiting the perspectives shared about the economy in the formation of monetary policy.

The statutory requirement for three classes of directors was intended to provide representation of both stockholding banks and the public. However, the existence of Class A and to a lesser extent Class B directors on the boards creates an appearance of a conflict of interest, particularly in matters involving supervision and regulation. Moreover, directors from all three classes could have past and current affiliations with financial institutions. These affiliations have given rise to relationships that pose reputational risk to the Reserve Banks. While director conflicts can be identified and managed, interconnectedness between directors and financial institutions cannot be eliminated; therefore, ongoing challenges remain. For example, the credibility of the Federal Reserve System will be affected by the perceived effectiveness of its ability to manage conflict issues. While the Federal Reserve System has recognized the importance of public perception and made changes to Reserve Bank governance practices, more could be done to increase the flow of information on the directors' roles to the public and strengthen controls. Specifically, greater transparency could assist the public in understanding the roles and functioning of the Reserve Bank boards, such as clarifying the limited nature of Reserve Bank directors' involvement in supervision and regulation operations with a statement in the Reserve Bank board bylaws could help to improve the public's confidence in Reserve Bank governance. While waivers are one way the Federal Reserve System mitigates conflicts involving Federal Reserve Board eligibility requirements, not all Reserve Banks have procedures for requesting a waiver from the Federal Reserve Board. Moreover, if waivers are granted, there is no requirement to make that information public. Failing to make the process and decisions more transparent can decrease confidence in the Federal Reserve System and has resulted in questions about the integrity of Reserve Banks' operations and the appearance of conflicts of interest.

Finally, while the Federal Reserve System has taken steps to increase transparency of governance practices as well as transparency overall, Reserve Bank governance practices were generally not as transparent as those of other central banks and financial institutions that we studied. In a time when the Federal Reserve System's emergency actions have resulted in relationships between Reserve Banks and directors and the relationships between directors and financial firms being questioned, more transparent governance practices are essential to the effective and credible functioning of the Reserve Banks and the Federal Reserve System as a whole. While the Federal Reserve System has taken some steps to increase the transparency of its governance practices, such as conducting quarterly press conferences after the FOMC meetings, additional actions such as making key governance documents easily accessible to the public could enhance transparency and protect organizational reputation. Moreover, without more public disclosure of governance arrangements, such as board of director bylaws and director eligibility and ethics policies, there may be continued concerns about Reserve Bank governance and the integrity of the Federal Reserve System.

RECOMMENDATIONS FOR EXECUTIVE ACTION

While the Federal Reserve System recently has made changes to Reserve Bank governance, it can take additional steps to strengthen controls designed to manage conflicts of interest involving Reserve Bank directors and increase public disclosure of directors' roles and responsibilities. As such, we recommend that the Chairman of the Federal Reserve Board take the following four actions:

- To help enhance economic and demographic diversity and broaden perspectives among Reserve Bank directors who are elected to represent the public, encourage all Reserve Banks to consider ways to broaden their pools of potential candidates for directors, such as including officers who are below the senior executive level at their organizations.
- To further promote transparency, direct all Reserve Banks to clearly document the roles and responsibilities of the directors, including

restrictions on their involvement in supervision and regulation activities, in their bylaws.

- As part of the Federal Reserve System's continued focus on strengthening governance practices, develop, document, and require all Reserve Banks to adopt a process for requesting waivers from the Federal Reserve Board director eligibility policy and ethics policy for directors. Further, consider requiring Reserve Banks to publicly disclose waivers that are granted to the extent disclosure would not violate a director's personal privacy.
- To enhance the transparency of Reserve Bank board governance, direct the Reserve Banks to make key governance documents, such as such as board of director bylaws, committee charters and membership, and Federal Reserve Board director eligibility policy and ethics policy, available on their websites or otherwise easily accessible to the public.

AGENCY COMMENTS AND OUR EVALUATION

We provided copies of this draft report to the Federal Reserve Board and the 12 Federal Reserve Banks for their review and comment. The Federal Reserve Board and the Reserve Banks provided written comments that we have reprinted in appendixes V and VI, respectively. The Federal Reserve Board and Reserve Banks also provided technical comments that we have incorporated as appropriate.

In its written comments, the Federal Reserve Board agreed that our recommendations have merit and to work to implement each of them. In particular, regarding our first recommendation on broadening the pools of candidates for the Reserve Bank directors, the Federal Reserve Board stated that, as we did in the report, several of the Reserve Banks are already considering qualified candidates who are not chief executives, as we have recommended, and the Federal Reserve Board will continue to explore ways to broaden the pool of candidates to increase diversity on Reserve Bank boards. We believe that diverse perspectives can enhance the formation of monetary policies.

With respect to our three recommendations to improve transparency, the Federal Reserve Board stated that it will work with the Reserve Banks to consider ways to more clearly include the directors' roles and responsibilities in the bylaws and the Federal Reserve System will continue to ensure that

Reserve Bank directors are fully aware of their roles and the policies that govern their positions on the Reserve Bank boards. Further, as we noted in the report, the Federal Reserve Board stated that in 2009 it adopted a process for Reserve Banks to request waivers from the eligibility policy and will consider adopting a process for waivers to the Guide to Conduct as well. In addition, it will consider making public any waivers granted, with due regard for protecting personal privacy. The Federal Reserve Board also stated that it will post various Reserve Bank director-related publications on its website and will work with the Reserve Banks to make available to the public other relevant governance documents and information. We believe that greater transparency could assist the public in understanding the roles and functioning of the Reserve Bank boards and help increase public confidence in the Federal Reserve System.

In its written comments, the Federal Reserve Banks stated that diversity and transparency are attributes valued and supported uniformly by all Reserve Banks. They stated that they welcomed our recommendation for Reserve Banks to consider ways to broaden the pool of potential candidates and reiterated that some Reserve Banks have already been considering qualified candidates who are not chief executives. They also agreed that transparency could be enhanced by our other recommendations.

If you or your staffs have any questions about this report, please contact Orice Williams Brown at williamso@gao.gov or (202) 512-8678. Contact points for our Offices of Congressional Relations and Public Affairs may be found on the last page of this report. GAO staff who made major contributions to this report are listed in appendix VII.

Orice Williams Brown
Managing Director,
Financial Markets and Community Investment

List of Congressional Addressees

The Honorable Harry Reid
Majority Leader
United States Senate

The Honorable Mitch McConnell
Minority Leader
United States Senate

The Honorable Tim Johnson
Chairman

The Honorable Richard C. Shelby
Ranking Member
Committee on Banking, Housing, and Urban Affairs
United States Senate

The Honorable Bernie Sanders
United States Senate

The Honorable John Boehner
Speaker of the House of Representatives

The Honorable Eric Cantor
Majority Leader
House of Representatives

The Honorable Nancy Pelosi
Minority Leader
House of Representatives

The Honorable Kevin McCarthy
House Majority Whip
House of Representatives

The Honorable Steny Hoyer
House Minority Whip
House of Representatives

The Honorable Spencer Bachus
Chairman

The Honorable Barney Frank
Ranking Member
Committee on Financial Services
House of Representatives

APPENDIX I: FEDERAL RESERVE EMERGENCY PROGRAMS AND RESERVE BANK INVOLVEMENT

The Federal Reserve Board Used Emergency and other Authorities to Authorize Liquidity Programs to Stabilize Markets and Institutions

Between late 2007 and early 2009, the Federal Reserve Board created more than a dozen new emergency programs to stabilize financial markets and provided financial assistance to avert the failures of a few individual institutions.[55] The Federal Reserve Board authorized most of this emergency assistance under emergency authority contained in section 13(3) of the Federal Reserve Act.[56] Three of the programs covered by this review—Term Auction Facility (TAF), dollar swap lines with foreign central banks, and the Agency Mortgage-Backed Securities (MBS) Purchase program—were authorized under other provisions of the Federal Reserve Act that do not require a determination that emergency conditions exist, although the swap lines and the Agency MBS Purchase Program did require authorization by the Federal Open Market Committee (FOMC). In many cases, the decisions by the Federal Reserve Board, the FOMC, and the Reserve Banks about the authorization, initial terms of, and implementation of the Federal Reserve System's emergency assistance were made over the course of only days or weeks as the Federal Reserve Board sought to act quickly to address rapidly deteriorating market conditions. As illustrated in table 5, the Federal Reserve Bank of New York (FRBNY) implemented most of these emergency activities under authorization from the Federal Reserve Board.

Table 5. List of Federal Reserve Emergency Programs and Reserve Banks That Conducted the Operations

Program and assistance	Description	Reserve Bank
Broad-based programs		
Term Auction Facility *(Dec. 12, 2007)*	Auctioned one-month and three-month discount window loans to eligible depository institutions	All 12 Reserve Banks
Dollar Swap Lines *(Dec. 12, 2007)*	Exchanged dollars with foreign central banks for foreign currency to help address disruptions in dollar funding markets abroad	FRBNY

Program and assistance	Description	Reserve Bank
Term Securities Lending Facility *(Mar. 11, 2008)*	Auctioned loans of U.S. Treasury securities to primary dealers against eligible collateral	FRBNY
Primary Dealer Credit Facility *(Mar. 16, 2008)*	Provided overnight cash loans to primary dealers against eligible collateral	FRBNY[a]
Asset-Backed Commercial Paper Money Market Mutual Fund Liquidity Facility *(Sept. 19, 2008)*	Provided loans to depository institutions and their affiliates to finance purchases of eligible asset-backed commercial paper from money market mutual funds	Federal Reserve Bank of Boston (FRBB)
Commercial Paper Funding Facility *(Oct. 7, 2008)*	Provided loans to a special-purpose vehicle to finance purchases of new issues of asset-backed commercial paper and unsecured commercial paper from eligible issuers	FRBNY
Money Market Investor Funding Facility *(Oct. 21, 2008, but never used)*	Created to finance the purchase of eligible short-term debt obligations held by money market mutual funds	FRBNY
Term Asset-Backed Securities Loan Facility *(Nov. 25, 2008)*	Provided loans to eligible investors to finance purchases of eligible asset-backed securities	FRBNY
Assistance to individual institutions		
Bear Stearns Companies, Inc. acquisition by JP Morgan Chase & Co.		
Bridge Loan *(Mar. 14, 2008)*	Overnight loan provided to JP Morgan Chase & Co. bank subsidiary, with which this subsidiary made a direct loan to Bear Stearns Companies, Inc.	FRBNY
Maiden Lane *(Mar. 16, 2008)*	Special purpose vehicle created to purchase approximately $30 billion of Bear Stearns's mortgage-related assets	FRBNY
American International Group, Inc. (AIG)		
Revolving Credit Facility *(Sept. 16, 2008)*	Revolving loan for the general corporate purposes of AIG and its subsidiaries, and to pay obligations as they came due	FRBNY
Securities Borrowing Facility *(Oct. 8, 2008)*	Provided collateralized cash loans to reduce pressure on AIG to liquidate residential mortgage-backed securities (RMBS) in its securities lending reinvestment portfolio	FRBNY
Maiden Lane II *(Nov.10, 2008)*	Special purpose vehicle created to purchase residential mortgage-backed securities from the securities lending portfolios of AIG subsidiaries	FRBNY

Table 5. (Continued)

Program and assistance	Description	Reserve Bank
Maiden Lane III *(Nov.10, 2008)*	Special purpose vehicle created to purchase coll-ateralized debt obligations on which AIG Finan-cial Products had written credit default swaps	FRBNY
Life Insurance Securitization *(March 2, 2009, but never used)*	Authorized to provide credit to AIG that would be repaid with cash flows from its life insurance businesses	FRBNY
Credit extensions to affiliates of some primary dealers *(Sept. 21, 2008)*	Loans provided to broker-dealer affiliates of four primary dealers on terms similar to those for Primary Dealer Credit Facility	FRBNY
Citigroup lending commitment *(Nov. 23, 2008)*	Commitment to provide nonrecourse loan to Citigroup against ring-fence assets if losses on asset pool reached $56.2 billion	FRBNY
Bank of America lending commitment *(Jan. 16, 2009)*	Commitment to provide nonrecourse loan facility to Bank of America if losses on ring-fence assets exceeded $18 billion (agreement never finalized)	Federal Res-erve Bank of Richmond (FRBR)
Open market operations		
Agency Mortgage-Backed Securities Purchase Program *(Nov. 25, 2008)*	Purchased agency mortgage-backed securities to provide support to mortgage and housing markets and to foster improved conditions in the financial markets more generally	FRBNY

Source: GAO summary of Federal Reserve System documents.

Notes: Dates in parentheses are the program announcement dates, and where relevant, the date the program or assistance was closed or terminated. On October 3, 2008, the Federal Reserve Board authorized the Direct Money Market Mutual Fund Lending Facility (DMLF) and rescinded this authorization 1 week later. DMLF was not implemented.

[a] PDCF was administered by FRBNY with operational assistance provided by the Federal Reserve Banks of Atlanta and Chicago .

In 2009, FRBNY, at the direction of the FOMC, began large-scale purchases of MBS issued by the housing government-sponsored enterprises, Fannie Mae and Freddie Mac, or guaranteed by Ginnie Mae.[57] Purchases of these agency MBS were intended to provide support to the mortgage and housing markets and to foster improved conditions in financial markets more generally. Most of the Federal Reserve Board's broad-based emergency programs closed on February 1, 2010. Figure 11 provides a timeline for the establishment, modification, and termination of Federal Reserve System emergency programs subject to this review.

In December 2007, the Federal Reserve Board Created TAF and Opened Swap Lines under Nonemergency Authorities to Address Global Strains in Interbank Lending Markets

In the months before the authorization of TAF and new swap line arrangements, which were the first of the emergency programs subject to this review, the Federal Reserve Board took steps to ease emerging strains in credit markets through its traditional monetary policy tools. In late summer 2007, sudden strains in term interbank lending markets emerged primarily due to intensifying investor concerns about commercial banks' actual exposures to various mortgage-related securities. The cost of term funding (loans provided at terms of 1 month or longer) spiked suddenly in August 2007, and commercial banks increasingly had to borrow overnight to meet their funding needs.[58] The Federal Reserve Board feared that the disorderly functioning of interbank lending markets would impair the ability of commercial banks to provide credit to households and businesses. To ease stresses in these markets, on August 17, 2007, the Federal Reserve Board made two temporary changes to the terms at which Reserve Banks extended loans through the discount window. First, it approved the reduction of the discount rate—the interest rate at which the Reserve Banks extended collateralized loans at the discount window—by 50 basis points.[59] Second, to address specific strains in term-funding markets, the Federal Reserve Board approved extending the discount window lending term from overnight to up to 30 days, with the possibility of renewal. According to a Federal Reserve Board study, this change initially resulted in little additional borrowing from the discount window.[60] In addition to the discount window changes, starting in September 2007, the FOMC announced a series of reductions in the target federal funds rate—the FOMC-established target interest rate that banks charge each other for loans. In October 2007, tension in term funding subsided temporarily. However, issues reappeared in late November and early December, possibly driven in part by a seasonal contraction in the supply of year-end funding.

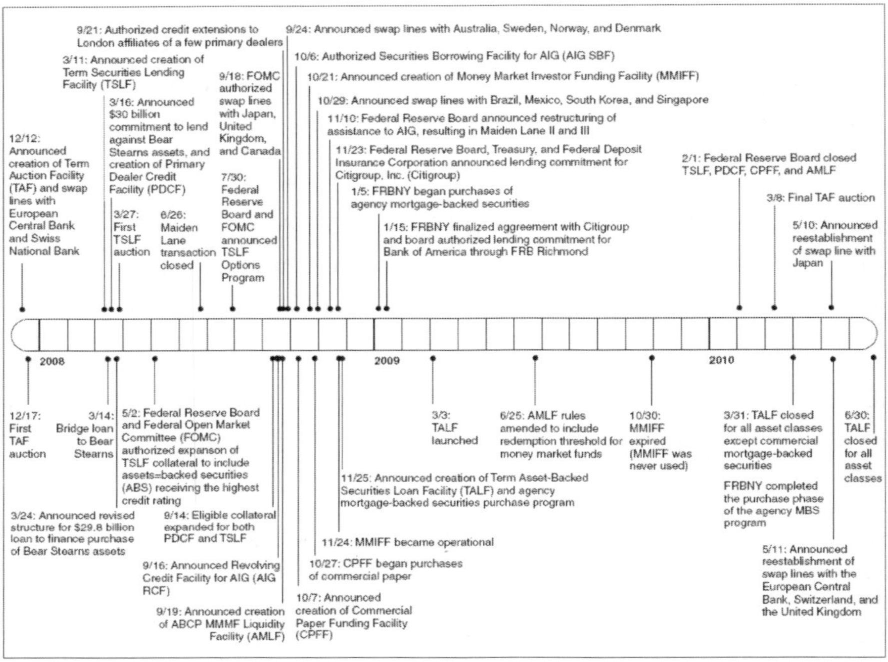

Source: Federal Reserve System documents and press releases.

Figure 11. Timeline of Federal Reserve Emergency Actions, December 2007–June 2010.

Term Auction Facility

On December 12, 2007, the Federal Reserve Board announced the creation of TAF to address continuing disruptions in U.S. term interbank lending markets. The Federal Reserve Board authorized Reserve Banks to extend credit through TAF by revising the regulations governing Reserve Bank discount window lending. TAF was intended to help provide term funding to depository institutions eligible to borrow from the discount window.[61] In contrast to the traditional discount window program, which loaned funds to individual institutions at the discount rate, TAF was designed to auction loans to many eligible institutions at once at a market-determined interest rate. Federal Reserve Board officials noted that one important advantage of this auction approach was that it could address concerns among eligible borrowers about the perceived stigma of discount window borrowing.[62] Federal Reserve Board officials noted that an institution might be reluctant to borrow from the discount window out of concern that its creditors and other counterparties might become aware of its discount window use and perceive it as a sign of distress. The auction format allowed banks to approach the Reserve Banks collectively rather than individually and obtain funds at an interest rate set by auction rather than at a premium set by the Federal Reserve Board.[63] Additionally, whereas discount window loan funds could be obtained immediately by an institution facing severe funding pressures, TAF borrowers did not receive loan funds until 3 days after the auction. For these reasons, TAF-eligible borrowers may have attached less of a stigma to auctions than to traditional discount window borrowing. The first TAF auction was held on December 17, 2007, with subsequent auctions occurring approximately every 2 weeks until the final TAF auction on March 8, 2010.

Dollar Swap Lines

Concurrent with the announcement of TAF, the FOMC announced the establishment of dollar swap arrangements with two foreign central banks to address similar disruptions in dollar funding markets abroad. In a typical swap line transaction, FRBNY exchanged dollars for the foreign central bank's currency at the prevailing exchange rate, and the foreign central bank agreed to buy back its currency (to "unwind" the exchange) at this same exchange rate at an agreed upon future date. The market for interbank funding in U.S. dollars is global, and many foreign banks hold U.S.-dollar-denominated assets and fund these assets by borrowing in U.S. dollars. In contrast to U.S. commercial banks, foreign banks did not hold significant U.S.-dollar deposits, and as a result, dollar funding disruptions were particularly acute for many foreign banks during the recent crisis. In December 2007, the European Central Bank and Swiss National Bank requested dollar swap arrangements with the Federal Reserve System to increase their ability to provide U.S. dollar loans to banks in their jurisdictions. Federal Reserve Board staff memorandums recommending that the FOMC approve these swap arrangements noted that continuing tension in dollar funding markets abroad could further exacerbate tensions in U.S. funding markets.[64] On December 6, 2007, the FOMC approved requests from the European Central Bank and Swiss National Bank and authorized FRBNY to establish temporary swap lines under section 14 of the Federal Reserve Act.[65] During 2008, the FOMC approved temporary swap lines with 12 other foreign central banks.[66] FRBNY's swap lines with the 14 central banks closed on February 1, 2010. In May 2010, to address the re-emergence of strains in dollar funding markets, FRBNY reopened swap lines with the Bank of Canada, the Bank of England, the European Central Bank, the Bank of Japan, and the Swiss National Bank through January 2011. On December 21, 2010, the FOMC announced an extension of these lines through August 1, 2011. On June 29, 2011, the Federal Reserve Board announced an extension of these swap lines through August 1, 2012.

In March 2008, the Federal Reserve Board Invoked Emergency Authority to Facilitate Sale of Bear Stearns and Expansion of Liquidity Support to Primary Dealers

In early March 2008, the Federal Reserve Board observed growing tension in the repurchase agreement markets—large, short-term collateralized funding markets—that many financial institutions rely on to finance a wide range of securities. Under a repurchase agreement, a borrowing institution generally acquires funds by selling securities to a lending institution and agreeing to repurchase the securities after a specified time at a given price. The securities, in effect, are collateral provided by the borrower to the lender. In the event of a borrower's default on the repurchase transaction, the lender would be able to take (and sell) the collateral provided by the borrower. Lenders typically will not provide a loan for the full market value of the posted securities, and the difference between the values of the securities and the loan is called a margin or haircut. This deduction is intended to protect the lenders against a decline in the price of the securities provided as collateral.[67] In early March, the Federal Reserve Board found that repurchase agreement lenders were requiring higher haircuts for loans against a range of securities and were becoming reluctant to lend against mortgage-related securities. As a result, many financial institutions increasingly had to rely on higher-quality collateral, such as U.S. Treasury securities, to obtain cash in these markets, and a shortage of such high-quality collateral emerged.[68] In March 2008, the Federal Reserve Board cited "unusual and exigent circumstances" in invoking section 13(3) of the Federal Reserve Act to authorize FRBNY to implement four emergency actions to address deteriorating conditions in these markets: (1) TSLF, (2) a bridge loan to Bear Stearns, (3) a commitment to lend up to $30 billion against Bear Stearns assets that resulted in the creation of Maiden Lane LLC, and (4) PDCF.

Term Securities Lending Facility

On March 11, 2008, the Federal Reserve Board announced the creation of the TSLF to auction 28-day loans of U.S. Treasury securities to primary dealers to increase the amount of high-quality collateral available for these dealers to borrow against in the repurchase agreement markets. Through competitive auctions that allowed dealers to bid a fee to exchange harder-to-finance collateral for easier-to-finance Treasury securities, TSLF was intended to promote confidence among lenders and to reduce the need for dealers to sell illiquid assets into the markets, which could have further depressed the prices of these assets and contributed to a downward price spiral.[69] TSLF auctioned loans of Treasury securities against two schedules of collateral. Schedule 1 collateral included treasuries, agency debt, and agency MBS collateral that FRBNY accepted in repurchase agreements for traditional open market operations with primary dealers.[70] Schedule 2 included schedule 1 collateral as well as a broader range of assets, including highly rated mortgage-backed securities.[71] The Federal Reserve Board determined that providing funding support for private mortgage-backed securities through the schedule 2 auctions fell outside the scope of FRBNY's authority to conduct its securities lending program under section 14 of the Federal Reserve Act. Accordingly, for the first time during this crisis, the Federal Reserve Board invoked section 13(3) of the Federal Reserve Act to authorize the extension of credit, in this case in the form of Treasury securities, to nondepository institutions—in this case, the primary dealers. As discussed later in this appendix the Federal Reserve Board later expanded the range of collateral eligible for TSLF as the crisis intensified. TSLF closed on February 1, 2010.

Bridge Loan to Bear Stearns

Shortly following the announcement of TSLF, the Federal Reserve Board invoked its emergency authority for a second time to authorize an emergency loan to avert a disorderly failure of Bear Stearns.[72] TSLF was announced on March 11, 2008, and the first TSLF auction was held on March 27, 2008. Federal Reserve Board officials noted that although TSLF was announced to address market tensions affecting many firms, some market participants concluded that its establishment was driven by specific concerns about Bear Stearns. Over a few days, Bear Stearns experienced a run on its liquidity as many of its lenders grew concerned that the firm would suffer greater losses in the future and stopped providing funding to the firm, even on a fully secured basis with high- quality assets provided as collateral.[73] Late on Thursday, March 13, 2008, the senior management of Bear Stearns notified the Federal Reserve that it would likely have to file for bankruptcy protection the following day unless the Federal Reserve provided the firm with an emergency loan. The Federal Reserve Board feared that the sudden failure of Bear Stearns could have serious adverse impacts on markets in which Bear Stearns was a significant participant, including the repurchase agreements market. In particular, a Bear Stearns failure may have threatened the liquidity and solvency of other large institutions that relied heavily on short-term secured funding markets. On Friday, March 14, 2008, the Federal Reserve Board voted to authorize FRBNY to provide a $12.9 billion loan to Bear Stearns through JP Morgan Chase Bank, National Association, the largest bank subsidiary of JP Morgan Chase & Co. (JPMC), and to accept $13.8 billion of Bear Stearns assets as collateral.[74] This back-to-back loan transaction was repaid on Monday, March 17, 2008, with almost $4 million of interest. This emergency loan enabled Bear Stearns to avoid bankruptcy and continue to operate through the weekend. This provided time for potential acquirers, including JPMC, to assess Bear Stearns's financial condition and for FRBNY to prepare a new liquidity program, PDCF, to address strains that could emerge from a possible Bear Stearns bankruptcy announcement the following Monday. Federal Reserve Board and FRBNY officials hoped that bankruptcy could be averted by the announcement that a private sector firm would acquire Bear Stearns and stand behind its liabilities when the markets reopened on the following Monday.

Maiden Lane LLC

On Sunday, March 16, 2008, the Federal Reserve Board announced that FRBNY would lend up to $30 billion against certain Bear Stearns assets to facilitate JPMC's acquisition of Bear Stearns. Over the weekend, JPMC had emerged as the only viable acquirer of Bear Stearns. In congressional testimony, Timothy Geithner, who was the President of FRBNY in March 2008, provided the following account:

"Bear approached several major financial institutions, beginning on March 13. Those discussions intensified on Friday and Saturday. Bear's management provided us with periodic progress reports about a possible merger. Although several different institutions expressed interest in acquiring all or part of Bear, it was clear that the size of Bear, the apparent risk in its balance sheet, and the limited amount of time available for a possible acquirer to conduct due diligence compounded the difficulty. Ultimately, only JPMorgan Chase was willing to consider an offer of a binding commitment to acquire the firm and to stand behind Bear's substantial short-term obligations."[75]

According to FRBNY officials, on the morning of Sunday, March 16, 2008, JPMC's Chief Executive Officer told FRBNY that the merger would be possible only if certain mortgage-related assets were taken off Bear Stearns's balance sheet. Negotiations between JPMC and FRBNY senior management resulted in a preliminary agreement under which FRBNY would make a $30 billion nonrecourse loan to JPMC collateralized by these Bear Stearns assets. A March 16, 2008, letter from then-FRBNY president Geithner to JPMC's Chief Executive Officer documented the terms of the preliminary agreement.[76]

Significant issues that threatened to unravel the merger agreement emerged soon after the announcement. Bear Stearns board members and shareholders thought JPMC's offer to purchase the firm at $2 per share was too low and threatened to vote against the merger. Perceived ambiguity in the terms of the merger agreement raised further concerns that JPMC could be forced to stand behind Bear Stearns's obligations even in the event that the merger was rejected. Moreover, some Bear Stearns counterparties stopped trading with Bear Stearns because of uncertainty about whether JPMC would honor certain Bear Stearns obligations. FRBNY also had concerns with the level of protection provided under the preliminary lending agreement, under which FRBNY had agreed to lend on a nonrecourse basis against risky collateral. The risks of an unraveled merger agreement included a possible Bear Stearns bankruptcy and losses for JPMC, which might have been legally required to stand behind the obligations of a failed institution. Recognizing the risk that an unraveled merger posed to JPMC and the broader financial markets, FRBNY officials sought to renegotiate the lending agreement.

During the following week, the terms of this agreement were renegotiated, resulting in the creation of a new lending structure in the form of Maiden Lane LLC. From March 17 to March 24, 2008, FRBNY, JPMC, and Bear Stearns engaged in dual track negotiations to address each party's concerns with the preliminary merger and lending agreements. On March 24, 2008, FRBNY and JPMC agreed to a new lending structure that incorporated greater loss protections for FRBNY. Specifically, FRBNY created a special-purpose vehicle (SPV), Maiden Lane LLC, that used proceeds from a $28.82 billion FRBNY senior loan and a $1.15 billion JPMC subordinated loan to purchase Bear Stearns assets.

Primary Dealer Credit Facility

While one team of Federal Reserve Board and FRBNY staff worked on options to avert a Bear Stearns failure, another team worked to ready PDCF for launch by Monday, March 17, 2008, when Federal Reserve Board officials feared a Bear Stearns bankruptcy announcement might trigger runs on the liquidity of other primary dealers. The liquidity support from TSLF would not become available until the first TSLF auction later in the month. On March 16,

2008, the Federal Reserve Board announced the creation of PDCF to provide overnight collateralized cash loans to the primary dealers. FRBNY quickly implemented PDCF by leveraging its existing legal and operational infrastructure for its existing repurchase agreement relationships with the primary dealers.[77] Although the Bear Stearns bankruptcy was averted, PDCF commenced operation on March 17, 2008, and in its first week extended loans to 10 primary dealers. Bear Stearns was consistently the largest PDCF borrower until June 2008. Eligible PDCF collateral initially included investment-grade corporate securities, municipal securities, and asset-backed securities, including mortgage-backed securities. The Federal Reserve Board authorized an expansion of collateral types eligible for PDCF loans later in the crisis. This program was terminated on February 1, 2010.

In Fall 2008, the Federal Reserve Board Modified Existing Programs and Launched Additional Programs to Support other Key Markets

In September 2008, the bankruptcy of Lehman Brothers triggered an intensification of the financial crisis, and the Federal Reserve Board modified the terms for its existing liquidity programs to address worsening conditions. On September 14, 2008, shortly before Lehman Brothers announced it would file for bankruptcy, the Federal Reserve Board announced changes to TSLF and PDCF to provide expanded liquidity support to primary dealers. Specifically, the Federal Reserve Board announced that TSLF-eligible collateral would be expanded to include all investment-grade debt securities and PDCF-eligible collateral would be expanded to include all securities eligible to be pledged in the triparty repurchase agreements system, including noninvestment grade securities and equities.[78] In addition, TSLF schedule 2 auctions would take place weekly rather than only biweekly. On September 21, 2008, the Federal Reserve Board announced that it would extend credit—on terms similar to those applicable for PDCF loans—to the U.S. and London broker-dealer subsidiaries of Merrill Lynch & Co. (Merrill Lynch), Goldman Sachs Group Inc. (Goldman Sachs), and Morgan Stanley to provide support to these subsidiaries as they became part of bank holding companies that would be regulated by the Federal Reserve System.[79] On September 29, 2008, the Federal Reserve Board also announced expanded support through TAF and the dollar swap lines. Specifically, the Federal Reserve Board doubled the amount of funds that would be available in each TAF auction cycle from $150 billion to $300 billion, and the FOMC authorized a $330 billion expansion of the swap line arrangements with foreign central banks.

In the months following Lehman's bankruptcy, the Federal Reserve Board authorized several new liquidity programs under section 13(3) of the Federal Reserve Act to provide support to other key funding markets, such as the commercial paper and the asset-backed security markets. In contrast to earlier emergency programs that represented relatively modest extensions of established Federal Reserve System lending or open market operation activities, these newer programs incorporated more novel design features and targeted new market participants with which the Reserve Banks had not historically transacted. As was the case with the earlier programs, many of these newer programs were designed and launched under extraordinary time constraints as the Federal Reserve Board sought to address rapidly deteriorating market conditions. In order of their announcement, these programs included (1) Asset- Backed Commercial Paper Money Market Mutual Fund Liquidity Facility (AMLF) to provide liquidity support to money market mutual funds (MMMF) in meeting redemption demands from investors and to foster liquidity in the asset-backed commercial paper (ABCP) market, (2) Commercial Paper Funding Facility (CPFF) to provide a liquidity backstop to eligible issuers of commercial paper, (3) the Money Market Investor Funding Facility (MMIFF) to serve as an additional backstop for MMMFs, and (4) the Term Asset-Backed Securities Loan Facility (TALF) to assist certain securitization markets that supported the flow of credit to households and businesses.

Asset-Backed Commercial Paper Money Market Mutual Fund Liquidity Facility

On September 19, 2008, the Federal Reserve Board authorized FRBB to establish AMLF to provide liquidity support to MMMFs facing redemption pressures.[80] According to FRBB staff, the processes and procedures to implement AMLF were designed over the weekend before FRBB commenced operation of AMLF on September 22, 2008. MMMFs were a major source of short-term credit for financial institutions, including through MMMFs' purchases and holdings of ABCP. ABCP continued to be an important source of funding for many businesses.[81] Following the announcement that a large MMMF had "broken the buck"—net asset value fell below $1 per share—as a result of losses on Lehman's commercial paper, other MMMFs faced a large wave of redemption requests as investors sought to limit their potential exposures to the financial sector. The Federal Reserve Board was concerned that attempts by MMMFs to raise cash through forced sales of ABCP and other assets into illiquid markets could further depress the prices of these assets and exacerbate strains in short-term funding markets. AMLF's design, which relied on intermediary borrowers to use Reserve Bank loans to fund the same-day purchase of eligible ABCP from MMMFs, reflected the need to overcome practical constraints in lending to MMMFs directly. According to Federal Reserve System officials, MMMFs would have had limited capacity to borrow directly from the Reserve Banks in amounts that would be sufficient to meet redemption requests because of statutory and fund- specific limitations on fund borrowing. To quickly support the MMMF market, the Federal Reserve Board authorized loans to entities that conduct funding and custodial activities, which include holding and administering the accounts with MMMF assets, with MMMFs to fund the purchase of ABCP from MMMFs. Eligible borrowers were identified as discount-window-eligible depository institutions (U .S. depository institutions and U.S. branches and agencies of foreign banks) and U.S. bank holding companies and their U.S. broker-dealer affiliates.[82] The interest rate on AMLF loans was lower than the returns on eligible ABCP, providing incentives for eligible intermediary borrowers to participate. AMLF closed on February 1, 2010.

Commercial Paper Funding Facility

On October 7, 2008, the Federal Reserve Board announced the creation of CPFF to provide a liquidity backstop to U.S. issuers of commercial paper. Commercial paper is an important source of short-term funding for U.S. financial and nonfinancial businesses.[83] CPFF became operational on October 27, 2008, and was operated by FRBNY. In establishing CPFF, FRBNY created an SPV that was to directly purchase new issues of eligible ABCP and unsecured commercial paper with the proceeds of loans it received from FRBNY for that purpose.[84] In the weeks leading up to CPFF's announcement, the commercial paper markets showed clear signs of strain: the volume of commercial paper outstanding declined, interest rates on longer-term commercial paper increased significantly, and increasing amounts of commercial paper were issued on an overnight basis as money market funds and other investors became reluctant to purchase commercial paper at longer-dated maturities.[86]

During this time, MMMFs faced a surge of redemption demands from investors concerned about losses on presumably safe instruments. The Federal Reserve Board concluded that disruptions in the commercial paper markets, combined with tension in other credit markets, threatened the broader economy as many large commercial paper issuers promoted the flow of credit to households and businesses. By standing ready to purchase eligible commercial paper, CPFF was intended to eliminate much of the risk that commercial paper issuers would be unable to issue new commercial paper to replace their maturing commercial paper obligations. By reducing this risk, CPFF was expected to encourage investors to continue or resume their purchases of commercial paper at longer maturities. CPFF closed on February 1, 2010.

Money Market Investor Funding Facility

On October 21, 2008, the Federal Reserve Board authorized FRBNY to work with the private sector to create MMIFF to serve as an additional backstop for MMMFs. MMIFF complemented AMLF by standing ready to purchase a broader range of short-term debt instruments held by MMMFs, including certificates of deposit and bank notes. MMIFF's design featured a complex lending structure through which five SPVs would purchase eligible instruments from eligible funds. In contrast to other Federal Reserve Board programs that created SPVs, MM IFF SPVs were set up and managed by private sector entities. According to FRBNY staff, JPMC, in collaboration with other firms that sponsored large MMMFs, brought the idea for an MMIFF-like facility to FRBNY in early October 2008, FRBNY worked with JPMC to set up the MMIFF SPVs but did not contract directly with JPMC or the firm that managed the MMIFF program. While MMIFF became operational in late November 2008, it was never used.

Term Asset-Backed Securities Loan Facility

In November 2008, the Federal Reserve Board authorized FRBNY to create TALF to reopen the securitization markets in an effort to improve access to credit for consumers and businesses.[86] During the recent financial crisis, the value of many asset-backed securities (ABS) dropped precipitously, bringing originations in the securitization markets to a virtual halt. Problems in the securitization markets threatened to make it more difficult for households and small businesses to access the credit that they needed to, among other things, buy cars and homes and expand inventories and operations.[87] TALF provided nonrecourse loans to eligible U.S. companies and individuals in return for collateral in the form of securities that could be forfeited if the loans were not repaid.[88] TALF was one of the more operationally complex programs, and the first TALF subscription was not held until March 2009. In contrast to other programs that had been launched in days or weeks, TALF required several months of preparation to refine program terms and conditions and consider how to leverage vendor firms to best achieve TALF policy objectives. TALF closed on June 30, 2010.

In Late 2008 and Early 2009, the Federal Reserve Board Announced Its Participation in Government Assistance to Individual Institutions

In late 2008 and early 2009, the Federal Reserve Board again invoked its authority under section 13(3) of the Federal Reserve Act to authorize assistance to avert the failures of three institutions that it determined to be systemically significant (1) American International Group, Inc. (AIG); (2) Citigroup, Inc. (Citigroup); and (3) Bank of America Corporation (Bank of America).

AIG

In September 2008, the Federal Reserve Board and the Treasury determined through analysis of information provided by AIG and insurance regulators, as well as publicly available information, that market events could cause AIG to fail, which would pose systemic risk to financial markets. The Federal Reserve Board and subsequently Treasury took steps to ensure that AIG obtained sufficient liquidity and could complete an orderly sale of some of its operating assets and continue to meet its obligations. On September 16, 2008, one day after the Lehman Brothers bankruptcy announcement, the Federal Reserve Board authorized FRBNY to provide a revolving credit facility (RCF) of up to $85 billion to help AIG meet its obligations. The AIG RCF was created to provide AIG with a revolving loan that AIG and its subsidiaries could use to address strains on their liquidity. The announcement of this assistance followed a downgrade of the firm's credit rating, which had prompted collateral calls by its counterparties and raised concerns that a rapid failure of the company would further destabilize financial markets. Two key sources of AIG's difficulties were AIG Financial Products Corp. (AIGFP) and a securities lending program operated by insurance subsidiaries of AIG.[89] AIGFP faced growing collateral calls on credit default swaps it had written on collateralized debt obligations (CDO).[90] Meanwhile, AIG faced demands on its liquidity from securities lending counterparties who were returning borrowed securities and demanding that AIG return their cash collateral.

Despite the announcement of the AIG RCF, AIG's condition continued to decline rapidly in fall 2008.

On subsequent occasions, the Federal Reserve Board invoked section 13(3) of the Federal Reserve Act to authorize either new assistance or a restructuring of existing assistance to AIG.

- First, in October 2008, the Federal Reserve Board authorized the creation of the securities borrowing facility (SBF) to provide up to $37.8 billion of direct funding support to a securities lending program operated by AIG's domestic insurance companies. From October 8, 2008, through December 11, 2008, FRBNY provided cash loans to AIG's domestic life insurance companies, collateralized by investment grade debt obligations.
- In November 2008, as part of plans to restructure the assistance to AIG to further strengthen its financial condition, and once again avert the failure of the company, the Federal Reserve Board and Treasury restructured AIG's debt. Under the restructured terms, Treasury purchased $40 billion in shares of AIG preferred stock and the cash from the sale was used to pay down a portion of AIG's outstanding balance from the AIG RCF. The limit on the facility also was reduced to $60 billion, and other changes were made.
- Also in November 2008, the Federal Reserve Board authorized the creation of two SPVs—Maiden Lane II LLC and Maiden Lane III LLC—to purchase certain AIG-related assets. Similar to Maiden Lane LLC, these SPVs funded most of these asset purchases with a senior loan from FRBNY.[91] Maiden Lane II replaced the AIG SBF and served as a longer-term solution to the liquidity problems facing AIG's securities lending program. Maiden Lane III purchased the underlying CDOs from AIG counterparties in connection with the termination of credit default swap contracts issued by AIGFP and thus the elimination of liquidity drain from collateral calls on the credit default swaps sold by AIGFP.
- In March 2009, the Federal Reserve Board and Treasury announced plans to further restructure AIG's assistance. According to the Federal Reserve Board, debt owed by AIG on the AIG RCF would be reduced by $25 billion in exchange for FRBNY's receipt of preferred equity interests totaling $25 billion in two SPVs. AIG created both SPVs to hold the outstanding common stock of two life insurance company

subsidiaries—American Life Insurance Company and AIA Group Limited.[92]

- Also in March 2009, the Federal Reserve Board authorized FRBNY to provide additional liquidity to AIG by extending credit by purchasing a contemplated securitization of income from certain AIG life insurance operations. FRBNY staff said this life insurance securitization option was abandoned for a number of reasons, including that it would have required FRBNY to manage a long-term exposure to life insurance businesses with which it had little experience.[93]

Citigroup

On November 23, 2008, the Federal Reserve Board authorized FRBNY to provide a lending commitment to Citigroup as part of a package of coordinated actions by Treasury, FDIC, and the Federal Reserve Board to avert a disorderly failure of the company.[94] As discussed in our April 2010 report on Treasury's use of the systemic risk determination, Treasury, FDIC, and the Federal Reserve Board said they provided emergency assistance to Citigroup because they were concerned that the failure of a firm of Citigroup's size and interconnectedness would have had systemic implications.[95] FRBNY agreed to lend against the residual value of approximately $300 billion of Citigroup assets if losses on these assets exceeded certain thresholds. On the basis of analyses by the various parties and an outside vendor, FRBNY determined that it would be unlikely that losses on the Citigroup "ring-fence" assets would reach the amount at which FRBNY would be obligated to provide a loan.[96] At Citigroup's request, Treasury, FDIC, and FRBNY agreed to terminate this loss sharing agreement in December 2009. As part of the termination agreement, Citigroup agreed to pay a $50 million termination fee to FRBNY. FRBNY never provided a loan to Citigroup under this lending commitment.[97]

Bank of America

On January 15, 2009, the Federal Reserve Board authorized FRBR to provide a lending commitment to Bank of America. As with Citigroup, the Federal Reserve Board authorized this assistance as part of a coordinated effort with Treasury and FDIC to assist an institution that the agencies determined to be systemically important. The circumstances surrounding the agencies' decision to provide this arrangement for Bank of America, however, were somewhat different and were the subject of congressional hearings.[98] While the Citigroup loss-sharing agreement emerged during a weekend over which the agencies attempted to avert an impending failure of the firm, the agencies' discussions with Bank of America about a possible similar arrangement occurred over several weeks during which Bank of America was not facing imminent failure. According to Federal Reserve Board officials, possible assistance for Bank of America was first discussed in late December 2008 when Bank of America management raised concerns about the financial impact of completing the merger with Merrill Lynch, which was expected at the time to announce larger than anticipated losses (and did in fact announce these losses the following month). Following the January 1, 2009, completion of Bank of America's acquisition of Merrill Lynch, the Federal Reserve Board and the other agencies agreed to provide a loss-sharing agreement on selected Merrill Lynch and Bank of America assets to assure markets that unusually large losses on these assets would not destabilize Bank of America. On September 21, 2009, the agencies and FRBR terminated the agreement in principle to enter into a loss sharing agreement with Bank of America. The agreement was never finalized, and FRBR never provided a loan to Bank of America under this lending commitment. As part of the agreement to terminate the agreement in principle, Bank of America paid $57 million to FRBR in compensation for out-of-pocket expenses incurred by FRBR and an amount equal to the commitment fees required by the agreement.

In 2009 and 2010, FRBNY Executed Large-Scale Purchases of Agency MBS to Provide Broader Support to the Economy

On November 25, 2008, the FOMC announced that FRBNY would purchase up to $500 billion of agency mortgage-backed securities to support the housing market and the broader economy.[99] The FOMC authorized the Agency MBS program under its authority to direct open market operations under section 14 of Federal Reserve Act. By purchasing MBS securities with longer maturities, the Agency MBS program was intended to lower long-term interest rates and to improve conditions in mortgage and other financial markets. The Agency MBS program commenced purchases on January 5, 2009, a little more than a month after the initial announcement. FRBNY staff noted that a key operational challenge for the program was its size. FRBNY hired external investment managers to provide execution support and advisory services needed to help execute purchases on such a large scale. In March 2009, the FOMC increased the total amount of planned purchases from $500 billion to up to $1.25 trillion. The program executed its final purchases in March 2010 and settlement was completed in August 2010.

Most Programs Were Extended a Few Times before Closing in Early 2010

On several occasions, the Federal Reserve Board authorized extensions of its emergency loan programs, and most of these programs closed on February 1, 2010. For example, AMLF, PDCF, and TSLF were extended three times. The Federal Reserve Board cited continuing disruptions in financial markets in announcing each of these extensions. Table 6 provides a summary of the extensions for the emergency programs.

Table 6. Summary of Extensions for Broad-Based Emergency Programs

Programs extended	Date extension announced	Term of extension
AMLF, PDCF, and TSLF	December 2, 2008	Original expiration: January 30, 2009
		New expiration: April 30, 2009
AMLF, CPFF, MMIFF, PDCF, TSLF, and swap lines with foreign central banks	February 3, 2009	Planned expiration: April 30, 2009
		New expiration: October 30, 2009
AMLF, CPFF, PDCF, TSLF, and swap lines with foreign central banks	June 25, 2009	Planned expiration: October 30, 2009
		New expiration: February 1, 2010

Source: GAO analysis of Federal Reserve Board press releases and program terms and conditions.

Note: MMIFF was never used and the Federal Reserve Board allowed it to expire on October 30, 2009. In November 2008, TALF was authorized to make new loans until December 31, 2009, and the Federal Reserve Board later authorized an extension for new loans against most eligible collateral until March 31, 2010, and against one eligible collateral type until June 30, 2010. Other extensions of swap line arrangements were announced on May 2, 2008, and September 29, 2008. In May 2010, FRBNY reopened swap lines with the Bank of Canada, the Bank of England, the European Central Bank, the Bank of Japan, and the Swiss National Bank. These swap lines were initially set to expire on August 1, 2011. On June 29, 2011, the Federal Reserve Board announced an extension of these swap lines through August 1, 2012.

APPENDIX II: FEDERAL RESERVE BANK DIRECTOR SURVEY METHODOLOGY AND RESULTS

Federal Reserve Bank Directors Survey: Survey Methodology

We conducted a brief Web-based survey of all Federal Reserve Bank (FRB) directors that served in 2010. The purpose of this survey was to gather basic information from FRB directors to fulfill GAO's congressional mandate to assess Federal Reserve Bank governance. Specifically, the survey asked about each director's (1) educational and professional background; (2) roles and responsibilities as a FRB director; and (3) opinions on FRB governance. The survey questions and summary results can be found below.

We sent a survey to all 105 directors that served for the full year during 2010.[100] We received completed surveys from 91 directors (87 percent response rate). The web-based survey was administered from April 4, 2011, to May 6, 2011. Directors were sent an e-mail invitation to complete the survey on a GAO web server using a unique username and password. Nonrespondents received a reminder e-mail from GAO to complete the survey. We also contacted the corporate secretaries at every bank and asked them to encourage their directors to participate in the survey. Even though we received responses from a majority of directors in all 12 banks, it is possible some bias may exist in certain survey responses if characteristics of respondents differed from those of nonrespondents in ways that affect the responses (e.g., if any knew of a potential conflict of interest at their bank they may or may not be less likely to respond to the survey).

The practical difficulties of conducting any survey may introduce additional nonsampling errors, such as difficulties interpreting a particular question, which can introduce unwanted variability into the survey results. We took steps to minimize nonsampling errors by pretesting the questionnaire with three directors in February and March 2011. We conducted pretests to make sure that the questions were clear and unbiased and that the questionnaire did not place an undue burden on respondents. An independent reviewer within GAO also reviewed a draft of the questionnaire prior to its administration. We made appropriate revisions to the content and format of the questionnaire after the pretests and independent review. All data analysis programs were independently verified for accuracy.

Survey of Federal Reserve Bank Directors: Survey Questions and Results

Section I: Your Background

We are interested in learning about the breadth of experience that Federal Reserve Bank directors bring to their positions on the Board.

1. How many years have you served as a Federal Reserve Bank head office director?

Responses	Missing	Mean	Low	High
89	2	3.3483	1	9

2. Educational Background of Federal Reserve Bank directors.

Degrees	Number of Directors Reporting Degree Completed
Associate's degree (for example: AA, AS)	8
Bachelor's degree (for example: BA,BS)	80
At least one Advanced Degree (Master's, Professional, or Doctorate)[a]	55
Master's degree (for example: MA, MS, MBA)	42
Professional degree (for example: MD, DDS, JD)	17
Doctorate (for example: PhD, EdD)	4

[a] Some respondents may have more than one advanced degree.

3. Work experience of Federal Reserve Bank directors.

Industries	Number of Directors Reporting Experience in the Industry
Agriculture, Forestry, Fishing and Hunting	12
Mining, Quarrying, and Oil and Gas Extraction	9
Utilities	8
Construction	14
Manufacturing	25
Wholesale Trade	11
Retail Trade	16
Transportation and Warehousing	14

Industries	Number of Directors Reporting Experience in the Industry
Information (Publishing, Broadcasting, and Telecommunications)	2
Financial Services (directors who selected at least one of the following five categories)	56
Credit Intermediation and Related Activities	21
Securities, Commodity Contracts, and Other Financial Investments and Related Activities	21
Insurance Carriers and Related Activities	9
Funds, Trusts, and Other Financial Vehicles	23
Offices of bank or other holding companies/ Corporate, Subsidiary, and Regional Managing Offices	41
Real Estate and Rental and Leasing	16
Professional, Scientific, and Technical Services (Legal, accounting, consulting, design, advertising, and public relations services)	21
Administrative and Support and Waste Management and Remediation Services	2
Educational Services	10
Health Care or Social Assistance	10
Arts, Entertainment, and Recreation	5
Accommodation and Food Services	4
Public Administration	12

Note: This list of industries is based on the 2007 North American Industry Classification System (NAICS).

4. Do you currently serve on any other boards (i.e., nonprofit, private or public company boards)?

	Frequency	Percent
Yes	86	94.51
No	5	5.49

5. Has someone from your current employer served as a Federal Reserve Bank (FRB) board director in the past 10 years?

	Frequency	Percent
Yes	6	6.59
No	83	91.21
Not sure	2	2.2

Section II: Your Roles and Responsibilities as a FRB Director

We are interested in learning about your duties as a Federal Reserve Bank director.

6. As a FRB Director, which of the following do you primarily represent? (check only one box)

	Frequency	**Percent**
The public	56	61.54
Your business/company	3	3.3
Banks in your district	23	25.27
Other businesses/companies in your district	3	3.3
Other (please specify below):	6	6.59

Seven directors provided an open-ended response to describe who they represent. Four directors indicated that their constituencies included the public, their business or industry, and other businesses or industries in the district. The other three directors listed food manufacturing and private equity, labor, transportation, communications, construction, and the public sector, and civic leadership and the nonprofit sector as the industries that they represent.

7. The three principal functions of FRB directors are listed below. Within each of these principal functions, which activities have you been involved in at your FRB? (check one box per question)

Responsibility & Activities	**Yes**	**No**	**Not Checked**
i. Overseeing the management of the Reserve Banks and Branches, with directors using their outside experience and judgment			
• Appointing senior bank officers	62	27	2
• Reviewing and approving the final FRB budget	82	8	1
• Overseeing bank operations, such as cash and check clearing, or payment systems, etc.	57	29	5
• Making procurement decisions	13	72	6
ii. Participating in the formulation of national monetary and credit policies			
• Collecting information from business and community leaders on the status of the regional and local economy to share with the FRB Board and Bank President	89	1	1

Responsibility & Activities	Yes	No	Not Checked
• Submitting a written report on local economic conditions to the FRB Board and Bank President	21	64	6
• Presenting an oral report on local economic conditions to the FRB Board and Bank President	88	1	2
iii. Acting as a link between the Federal Reserve and the private sector			
• Giving speeches to local community groups	42	46	3
• Talking to smaller, informal groups about the Federal Reserve Bank's mission	72	19	0

8. How frequently do you communicate with the following Reserve Bank personnel while carrying out your official duties? (check one box per person)

Bank Official	Frequently		Occasionally		Infrequently/ as needed		Not at All		Not Checked	
	#	%	#	%	#	%	#	%	#	%
Bank President	52	57.14	30	32.97	9	9.89	0	0	0	0
First Vice President	42	46.15	35	38.46	13	14.29	1	1.1	0	0
Corporate Secretary	37	40.66	38	41.76	16	17.58	0	0	0	0
General Counsel	17	18.68	35	38.46	34	37.36	5	5.49	0	0
Ethics Officer (may be the same person who serves as Corporate Secretary or General Counsel)	8	8.79	32	35.16	39	42.86	11	12.09	1	1.1
Director of Research	17	18.68	41	45.05	24	26.37	7	7.69	2	2.2
Director of Supervision and Regulation	3	3.3	32	35.16	28	30.77	28	30.77	0	0
General Auditor	36	39.56	24	26.37	22	24.18	9	9.89	0	0
Other members of senior management	7	7.69	42	46.15	36	39.56	5	5.49	1	1.1
Other (please specify below):	4	4.4	2	2.2	7	7.69	8	8.79	70	76.92

In the open-ended question that asked directors to specify what "other" FRB staff with whom they interacted, directors listed the following staff members: assistants to senior management, executive vice president of operations, vice president of Information Technology, assistant general auditor, librarian, Federal Reserve Information Technology officers, members of the Federal Reserve Board, presidents of other Reserve Banks, other staff as questions arise, and vice president of Human Resources/Diversity.

9. In the past year, in your role as a director, have you been involved in any Division of Supervision and Regulation matters in which you did any of the following: (check one box per question)

Supervision and Regulation Activities	**Yes**	**No**	**Not Checked**
• Were involved in making decisions about specific banks that the FRB supervises?	0	91	0
• Received general information about the supervisory status of banks in the district?	35	56	0
• Received supervisory information about the status of any specific banks?	2	89	0
• Were involved in making personnel decisions about pay or promotion for employees in the Division of Supervision and Regulation?	21	69	1
• Were involved in making decisions about the budget for the Division of Supervision and Regulation?	22	68	1
• Had other involvement with the Division of Supervision and Regulation not described above?	6	85	0

GAO asked directors who answered "yes" to any of these questions to explain their answer. We analyzed the open ended answers for this question and no improper conflicts of interest were identified.

10. The following questions are about the FRB's code or standards of conduct for directors (code). Did you do any of the following? (check one box per question)

Standard of Conduct	Yes	No	Don't Remember	Not Checked
• Receive training on the code at your FRB at the beginning of your term in office?	90	0	1	0
• Receive training on the code in Washington, D.C. at the beginning of your term in office?	67	9	15	0
• Sign an oath of office at the beginning of your term agreeing to adhere to the code?	77	1	13	0
• Receive an annual briefing on the code of conduct by a member of the bank's senior management?	79	3	7	2
• Sign an annual certification agreeing to adhere to the code?	65	4	21	1

GAO asked directors who answered "no" to any of the above questions to provide an explanation. Four directors stated they were unable to attend the training in Washington, D.C. Two directors said they attended the training but did not receive training on the code of conduct and two other directors said they did not recall if they signed an annual certification.

11. Are you aware of any past or current conflicts of interest with any FRB directors in your district?

Aware of Conflicts	Frequency	Percent
Yes	5	5.49
No	86	94.51

GAO asked directors who responded "yes" to this question to explain the conflict and how it was resolved. Five directors provided responses to this open-ended question on the survey. Two of the responses described actual or potential conflicts of interest involving procurement matters and the directors recused themselves from voting on the matter. One of those directors also noted that the CEO of Lehman Brothers, Inc., resigned as a director because the company was requesting assistance from the FRB. Another described a director who resigned because he expressed a desire to be involved in a political campaign. One director declined a board position at another entity because of perceived conflicts of interest. Another director noted that the board was apprised of a potential conflict of interest between a branch director and FRB auditors, and that the situation was resolved and reported to the Audit Committee.

Section III: Your Opinions on FRB Governance

We are interested in learning about your views on how, if at all, Federal Reserve Bank governance practices could be strengthened.

12. In terms of Federal Reserve Bank governance, how would you strengthen achievement in the following areas, if at all? Please include examples of practices in your district or from other relevant board experience that may assist the Federal Reserve System in strengthening achievement in the following areas.
    a. Improve public representation on FRB Boards?
    b. Eliminate actual or potential conflicts of interest of Reserve Bank directors?
    c. Increase the availability of information useful for the formation and execution of monetary policy?
    d. Increase the effectiveness or efficiency of reserve banks?

The open-ended responses were analyzed and included as examples in the report when appropriate.

APPENDIX III: FEDERAL RESERVE BANKS BOARD COMMITTEES

The Reserve Bank boards use committees to help oversee the operations of the Reserve Banks and their branches. The Federal Reserve Board requires all Reserve Banks to have standing audit committees and as needed search committees for the selection and appointment of a president. The Reserve Banks use various other committees, including budget and governance committees.

Table 7. Federal Reserve Banks Board Committees

Federal Reserve Bank	Committee	Description
Boston		
	Audit Committee	Assists the board in overseeing the bank's internal audit function, external auditor, risk management program, and system of internal controls
	Nominating and Governance Committee	Assists the board by identifying and recommending candidates for open director positions, selecting members of board committees in accordance with the bylaws, and reviewing and recommending improvements to board governance practices
	Business Commitments and Performance Committee	Reviews and makes recommendations to the board regarding the bank's annual plan and budget, significant capital expenditures, and operating performance including centrally provided Federal Reserve System services affecting the bank
	Research and Regional Outreach Committee	Reviews and provides advice to the president on the economic research program and other activities of the Research Department, public and community affairs programs, and other outreach efforts undertaken by the bank
	Executive Committee	Subject to the supervision and control of the board, has the power, between meetings of the board, to direct the business of the bank, and to exercise all the power and authority vested by law in the board
New York		
	Audit and Operational Risk Committee	Assists the board in monitoring (1) the integrity of the financial statements of the bank, (2) the bank's external auditor's qualifications and independence, (3) the performance of the bank's internal audit function and external auditors, (4) internal controls and the measurement of operational risk, and (5) the compliance by the bank with legal and regulatory requirements
	Nominating and Corporate Governance Committee	Considers and makes recommendations concerning board and board committee membership; assigns board members to board committees; evaluates the performance of the board committees and their members; and reviews and revises the charters of board committees
	Management and Budget Committee	Reviews and endorses the bank's strategic plan, budget and self-evaluation of the bank's performance, prepared by bank management, prior to submission to the Board of Governors of the Federal Reserve System for action
	Executive Committee	Has the power to direct the business of the bank, and to exercise all the power and authority vested by law in the board insofar as such power and authority may lawfully be delegated to the Executive Committee

Table 7. (Continued)

Federal Reserve Bank	Committee	Description
Philadelphia		
	Audit Committee	Responsible for ensuring the effectiveness and independence of the internal audit function, as well as to provide assistance to the board of directors by ensuring that management maintains an effective system of internal control
	Nominating and Governance Committee	Responsible for reviewing, evaluating, and recommending changes to board practices; considering all matters of corporate governance; and supporting bank management in its cultivation of quality director candidates
	Management and Budget Committee	Responsible for reviewing operating targets and objectives, as well as the financial costs associated with their accomplishment
	Executive Committee	Has the power to direct the business of the bank, and to exercise all the power and authority vested by law in the board insofar as such power and authority may lawfully be delegated to the committee
Cleveland		
	Audit Review Committee	Has the primary responsibility for maintaining contact with the General Auditor and satisfying itself that appropriate audit programs and procedures are maintained by the Audit Department
	Corporate Governance Committee	Responsible for reviewing the bank's bylaws and governance-related management policies, as well as conducting the board's annual evaluation, reviewing compensation and performance plans for the president and first vice president, and assisting the board in the appointment of branch directors
	Operations/ Resource Committee	Responsible for assisting the board of directors in fulfilling its oversight responsibilities related to strategy and budget, major personnel policies, and initiatives including diversity and inclusion, talent management and compensation, and overall bank operations. The committee also serves as the oversight body responsible for ensuring the bank has implemented an effective enterprise risk management program and practices
	Executive Committee	Has the power to direct the affairs of the bank and to exercise all the power and authority vested by law in the board
Richmond		
	Audit Committee	Has the primary responsibility for maintaining contact with the General Auditor and shall satisfy itself that appropriate audit programs and procedures are maintained by the Audit Department and that the General Auditor has proper official status and sufficient staff, both numerically and qualitatively, to discharge the responsibilities of the General Auditor's office

Federal Reserve Bank	Committee	Description
	Committee on Planning & Operations	Oversees the strategic plan and strategic planning process and budget, budget process, and financial performance
	Committee on Human Resources	Meets with the president, first vice president, and senior officer in charge of Human Resources to develop recommendations concerning adjustments in executive vice president and senior vice president salary structures. The committee also reviews and approves official executive vice president and senior vice president appointments, promotions, and other recommendations made by the president and first vice president before approval by the board of directors
	Executive Committee	Has the power (1) to establish from time to time, as required by law, rates of discount and purchase for each class of paper, subject to review and determination of the Board of Governors of the Federal Reserve System and (2) to exercise generally between meetings of the board all other powers of the board of directors, except as may be otherwise provided in the bylaws
Atlanta		
	Audit Committee	Performs functions necessary to assess the effectiveness and independence of the bank's internal and external audit function in providing an independent and objective assessment of the bank's risk management, control, and governance processes
	Operations Oversight Committee	Provides board oversight and linkage to the district and national business operations of the bank
	Executive Committee	Has the power to direct the business of the bank, including the power to establish discount rates and to exercise all powers and authority vested by law in the board of directors in so far as such powers and authority may lawfully be delegated to the Executive Committee
Chicago		
	Audit Committee	Responsible for assessing the effectiveness and independence of the bank's internal audit function and for those other matters specified in the Audit Committee charter
	Governance and Human Resources Committee	Finds and encourages qualified individuals to run for elected director positions or agree to have their names submitted to the Board of Governors of the Federal Reserve System or the board for appointed positions and considers matters of corporate governance and human resources and for those matters specified in the Governance and Human Resources Committee charter
	System Acti-vities, Bank	Oversees the bank's local and national business operations to ensure adherence to strategies and standards set for the

Table 7. (Continued)

Federal Reserve Bank	Committee	Description
	Operations and Risk Committee	Federal Reserve System, the bank's operations, performance and budget and for those matters specified in the committee charter
	Executive Committee	Available to act for the board between board meetings or whenever a quorum is not present at a board meeting
St. Louis		
	Audit Committee	Has the primary responsibility for maintaining contact with the General Auditor, and shall satisfy itself that appropriate audit programs and procedures are maintained, and that the General Auditor has proper official status and sufficient staff, both numerically and qualitatively, to discharge the responsibilities of the office
	Governance and Operations Committee	Subject to the supervision and control of the board of directors, shall consider matters pertaining to the material activities of the bank, its human resources policies and practices, and shall review the practices of the board of directors and its committees
	Executive Committee	Has the power to direct the business of the bank and to excise all the power and authority vested by law in the board of directors
Minneapolis		
	Audit Committee	Assesses the effectiveness and independence of the internal audit function and reports the results of those assessments to the board of directors
	Nominating Committee	Considers candidates for Board of Governors-appointed directorships at Minneapolis and the two Board of Governors-appointed directorships at the Helena branch
	Executive Committee	Has the general power, during intervals between meetings of the bank board, to supervise and control the business of the bank, and the power, subject to review and determination of the Board of Governors of the Federal Reserve System, to set the discount rates of the bank
	Budget/ Evaluation Committee	Primary responsibility is to review in detail the Bank's annual planning and budgeting prior to consideration by the board of directors. The committee also serves to acquaint directors with Board of Governors of the Federal Reserve System's' evaluations of bank performance and with the rationale for bank responses to such evaluations, including resource tradeoffs and unique needs of the district
Kansas City		
	Audit Committee	Primary purpose is to assist the board in fulfilling its oversight responsibilities relating to (1) the integrity of the bank's financial statements, (2) the evaluation and retention

Federal Reserve Bank	Committee	Description
		of the independent auditor, (3) the performance of the bank's Internal Audit function, (4) the bank's compliance with its Code of Conduct, and (5) the bank's risk management policies and practices
	Buildings Committee	Provides general oversight on behalf of the bank's board of directors for significant construction or renovation projects undertaken by the bank
	Compensation Committee	Responsible for approving the limits of the bank's compensation program subject to such approvals as may be required by the Board of Governors of the Federal Reserve System
	Search Committee	Responsible for leading the search process to identify qualified candidates for the position of president, chief executive officer, and first vice president
	Executive Committee	Has the authority to conduct the business of the bank in the interims between meetings of the board of directors, including the authority to establish rates of discount pursuant to the provisions of the Federal Reserve Act
Dallas		
	Audit Committee	Provides assistance to the board of directors in fulfilling their responsibility to ensure that management maintains an effective system of internal control
	Budget, Planning and Compensation Committee	Has the authority to review and comment on the bank's budget document, which includes the bank's general approach to salary administration for officers and employees, prior to its presentation to the full board of directors
	Nominating and Governance Committee	Provides assistance to the board of directors in fulfilling its responsibilities on matters relating to (1) guiding the board in an annual review of the board's performance and the performance of board committees, (2) assisting the identification of candidates qualified to become Class B and Class C directors, and (3) recommending to the board the director nominees for each committee of the board
	Executive Committee	Has the power to conduct the business of the bank in the interims between meetings of the board of directors, including the power to establish from time to time rates of discount in pursuance of the provisions of Section 14 of the Federal Reserve Act
San Francisco		
	Audit & Risk Management Committee	Assists the board of directors in fulfilling its oversight responsibility to ensure that management achieves organizational objectives principally by promoting and evaluating the effectiveness and independence of the internal audit function
	Bank Performance Committee	Reviews the bank's strategic direction and the performance of the bank, the president, and the first vice president on behalf of the board of directors

Table 7. (Continued)

Federal Reserve Bank	Committee	Description
	Community & Public Affairs Committee	Assists the bank in carrying out its outreach and education programs
	Executive Committee	Has the power to conduct the business of the bank, and to exercise all the power and authority vested by law in the Board insofar as such power and authority may lawfully be delegated to the committee

Source: GAO summary of various Reserve Bank bylaws and committee charters (2009-2011) and Reserve Bank officials.

Appendix IV: Ten Largest Domestic Bank Holding Companies by Total Asset Size as of December 31, 2010

Domestic bank holding companies	Total Assets as of 12/31/10 (Dollars in thousands)
1. Bank of America Corporation	$2,268,347,377
2. JPMorgan Chase & Co.	$2,117,605,000
3. Citigroup Inc.	$1,913,902,000
4. Wells Fargo & Company	$1,258,128,000
5. The Goldman Sachs Group, Inc.	$911,330,000
6. Morgan Stanley	$807,698,000
7. Metlife, Inc.	$730,905,863
8. U.S. Bancorp	$307,786,000
9. The PNC Financial Services Group, Inc.	$264,414,112
10. The Bank of New York Mellon Corporation	$247,222,000

Source: GAO analysis of data from the National Information Center.

End Notes

[1] For this report, we use Federal Reserve Board to refer to the federal agency and Federal Reserve System to refer collectively to the federal agency and the Reserve Banks.

[2] Pub. L. No. 111-203, Title XI, § 1109(b), 121 Stat. 1376, 2127 (2010).

[3] This report addresses the governance practices involving Reserve Bank directors. The governance structure of the Federal Reserve System, that is, the structure of a central,

governmental agency, with 12 regional Reserve Banks, is not within the scope of this report.

[4] Beginning in 2007, EEOC divided the "officials and managers" category into two subcategories. The first one, "executive/senior level officials and managers," includes individuals who reside in the highest levels of organizations and plan, direct and formulate policies, set strategy, and provide the overall direction of enterprises/organizations for the development and delivery of products or services, within the parameters approved by boards of directors or other governing bodies. The second category, "first/mid-level officials and managers," includes individuals who receive directions from executive/senior level management, and oversee and direct the delivery of products, services, or functions at group, regional, or divisional levels of organizations.

[5] Generally, private employers with fewer than 100 employees and certain federal contractors who employ fewer than 50 employees are not required to submit EEO-1 reports to EEOC. Although the EEO-1 data do not include these smaller firms, the data do allow for the characterization of workforce diversity for firms with 100 or more employees because of EEOC's annual reporting requirement.

[6] The Dodd-Frank Act also required us to report on issues related to the Federal Reserve emergency programs. See GAO, *Federal Reserve System: Opportunities Exist to Strengthen Policies and Processes for Managing Emergency Assistance*, GAO-11-696 (Washington, D.C.: July 21, 2011).

[7] Federal Reserve Act of 1913, Pub. L. No. 63-43, 38 Stat. 251 (1913).

[8] The Dodd-Frank Act includes provisions that expand the roles and responsibilities of the Federal Reserve System. First, the act authorizes the Federal Reserve Board to regulate nonbank financial companies designated as systemically significant by a newly created Financial Stability Oversight Council (FSOC) and to regulate savings and loan holding companies (thrift holding companies). FSOC is chaired by the Secretary of the Treasury, and its membership includes the Chairman of the Federal Reserve Board and the heads of the other federal financial regulators. In addition, the act consolidated many federal consumer protection responsibilities into a new independent Bureau of Consumer Financial Protection within the Federal Reserve System. The bureau is commonly known as CFPB. However, CFPB is an independent agency not under the supervision or direction of the Federal Reserve Board.

[9] The FOMC has directed the Federal Reserve Bank of New York (FRBNY) to execute monetary policy operations.

[10] Section 11 B of the Federal Reserve Act, codified at 12 U.S.C. § 248b.

[11] Until recently, the Federal Reserve Act provided that Reserve Bank presidents were to be appointed by their boards of directors, with Federal Reserve Board approval. Pursuant to section 1107 of the Dodd-Frank Act, however, only Class B and Class C directors are authorized to appoint Reserve Bank presidents, again with the approval of the Federal Reserve Board. Because section 4(4) of the Federal Reserve Act requires the first vice president to be appointed in the same manner as the president, this requirements also applies to first vice presidents.

[12] The groups' capitalization ranges are determined by each Reserve Bank and vary among Reserve Banks.

[13] The Federal Funds Rate is the interest rate at which depository institutions lend balances to each other overnight.

[14] The discount rate is the interest rate charged to commercial banks and other depository institutions on loans they receive from their regional Reserve Bank's discount window.

[15] The Federal Reserve Act also authorizes the Federal Reserve Board to remove any officer or director of a Reserve Bank.

[16] The Federal Reserve Board must also approve the budget of each Reserve Bank pursuant to the requirement that it exercise general supervision over each Reserve Bank.

[17] Until recently, the Federal Reserve Act provided that Reserve Bank presidents were to be appointed by their boards of directors, with Federal Reserve Board approval. However, pursuant to section 1107 of the Dodd-Frank Act, only Class B and Class C directors are authorized to appoint Reserve Bank presidents, again with the approval of the Federal Reserve Board.

[18] Individuals who responded to the question on race by indicating only one race are included in the race-alone population or the groups that reported only one race category.

[19] Pub. L. No. 95-188, §202, 91 Stat. 1387 (1977).

[20] We removed duplicate observations for directors that served for more than one year during this time frame to create a dataset of unique directors for the purposes of this analysis.

[21] Although there is no legal limit on the number of terms a director can serve, the Federal Reserve Board recommends that the Reserve Banks follow a limit of two consecutive appointments for a given director. For this analysis, we counted directors serving multiple years only once.

[22] One branch (Buffalo) closed during this period, which decreased the number of branch directors.

[23] Of the 105 surveyed, 91 responded to the survey overall. However, the number of respondents varied by question.

[24] Under Federal Reserve Board policy, Class B and Class C directors are prohibited from having a current affiliation with certain institutions, including among other things, banks or bank holding companies, branches or agencies of foreign banks, thrift institutions, credit unions or subsidiaries of any such company or entity.

[25] The industry list used in the survey was based on the 2007 North American Industry Classification System (NAICS).

[26] According to the Federal Reserve Board, only member banks vote for directors, so it almost never happens that a nonmember bank representative becomes a director.

[27] GAO, *Financial Services Industry: Overall Trends in Management-Level Diversity and Diversity Initiatives, 1993-2008,* GAO-10-736T (Washington, D.C.: May 1 2, 2010).

[28] The manual clarifies voting procedures for electing Class A and Class B directors and provides sample ballot forms and voting instructions.

[29] An annual listing of the top 500 U.S. corporations compiled by *Fortune* magazine. The companies are ranked by 12 indexes, among them revenues; profits; assets; stockholders' equity; market value; profits as a percentage of revenues, assets, and stockholders' equity; earnings per share growth over a 10-year span; total return to investors in the year; and the 10-year annual rate of total return to investors.

[30] Directors are compensated for travel expenses and given a daily fee for attendance at directors meetings, committee meetings, or while otherwise engaged in official business for the bank. The daily fee ranges from $100 to $300 depending on whether they are chairmen, deputy chairmen, or directors. Also, head office directors receive an annual retainers ranging from $2,000 to $5,000 depending on whether they are chairmen, deputy chairmen or directors.

[31] The 2010 National Association of Corporate Directors Annual Survey of Public Company Governance found that one-third of companies limited the number of boards that a director can serve on.

[32] GAO-11-696.

[33] Although there is no statutory prohibition, there is a Federal Reserve Board policy that prohibits individuals that hold bank holding company stocks from serving as Class C directors.

[34] Among these authorities was Section 13(3) of the Federal Reserve Act of 1913, which, at the time of the authorizations, allowed the Federal Reserve Board, in "unusual and exigent circumstances," to authorize any Reserve Bank to extend credit to individuals, partnerships, or corporations under certain conditions.

[35] The Term Auction Facility—one of the first emergency facilities created—auctioned one-month and three-month discount window loans to eligible depository institutions. For a more a detailed discussion of this and other emergency programs, see appendix I.

[36] FRBNY's AORC is appointed by its board of directors to assist the board in monitoring (1) the integrity of the financial statements of the Reserve Bank, (2) the Reserve Bank's external auditor's qualifications and independence, (3) the performance of the Reserve Bank's internal audit function and external auditors, (4) internal controls and the measurement of operational risk, and (5) the compliance by the Reserve Bank with legal and regulatory requirements. The Audit and Operational Risk Committee also assesses the effectiveness of (2), (3), (4), and (5).

[37] GAO-11-696, 81.

[38] A clearing bank is a commercial bank that facilitates payment and settlement of financial transactions, such as check clearing or matching trades between the sellers and buyers of securities and other financial instruments and contracts.

[39] The Primary Dealer Credit Facility provided overnight cash loans to primary dealers against eligible collateral.

[40] The Federal Reserve System is responsible for the supervision and regulation of state-chartered banks that are members of the Federal Reserve, all bank holding companies, and certain other institutions that are in engaged in a foreign banking business and the United States activities of foreign banks. The Reserve Banks' Supervision and Regulation Department examines these institutions for safety and soundness under authority delegated from the Federal Reserve Board, and the Federal Reserve Board writes and issues regulations and guidelines regarding the structure and conduct of the financial institutions.

[41] 18 U.S.C. § 208; 5 C.F.R. Parts 2635, 2640.

[42] See 5 C.F.R. § 2635.402(c)-(e).

[43] 5 C.F.R. § 2640.203(h).

[44] 60 Fed. Reg. 47,208, 47,220 (Sept. 11, 1995).

[45] For example, section 4(8) of the Federal Reserve Act requires the board of directors to administer the affairs of the Reserve Bank fairly and impartially and without discrimination in favor of or against any member bank or banks.

[46] In 2009, the Federal Reserve Board formalized a waiver process in the Eligibility, Qualifications, and Rotation Policy. The policy provides, among other things, that in rare and exigent circumstances, the Board of Governors may approve a request from a Reserve Bank for a waiver. The Reserve Bank may submit a written request for a waiver upon a vote of the board of directors on whether to recommend a waiver. The Federal Reserve Board must approve the Reserve Bank's waiver request in order for it to become effective.

[47] Prior to the Dodd-Frank Act, all members of the board of directors of a Reserve Bank were authorized to appoint the Reserve Bank president, with the final selection subject to the approval of the Federal Reserve Board. Pursuant to section 1107 of the Dodd-Frank Act, however, only Class B and Class C directors are authorized to appoint Reserve Bank presidents, again with the approval of the Federal Reserve Board.

[48] Pursuant to section 1 2A of the Federal Reserve Act, in addition to the governors of the Federal Reserve Board, the FOMC's members are five representatives of the Reserve Banks who are to be either presidents or vice presidents of the banks. The president of FRBNY serves on a continuous basis, and the other members are elected annually on a rotating basis.

[49] GAO, *Corporate Governance: NCUA's Controls and Related Procedures for Board Independence and Objectivity Are Similar to Other Financial Regulators, but Opportunities Exist to Enhance Its Governance Structure*, GAO-07-72R (Washington, D.C.: Nov. 30, 2006).

[50] Organisation for Economic Co-operation and Development, Principles of Corporate Governance, 2004. Available at www.oecd.org/daf/corporateaffairs/principles/text

[51] 12 U.S.C. § 1427(a)(2).

[52] Item 407(d)(3)(i) of Regulation S-K.

[53] GAO, *Federal Oversight: The Need of Good Governance, Transparency, and Accountability,* GAO-07-788CG (Washington, D.C.: Apr. 16, 2007).

[54] World Bank, *Annual Review of Development Effectiveness: Getting Results* (Washington, D.C., 2006); International Monetary Fund, *Code of Good Practices on Transparency in Monetary and Financial Policies*, 1999, available at http://www.imf.org/external/np/mae/mft/code/index.htm; and Organisation for Economic Co-operation and Development, *Principles of Corporate Governance*, 2004, available at www.oecd.org/daf/corporateaffairs/principles/text.

[55] For this appendix, we use Federal Reserve Board to refer to the Board of Governors of the Federal Reserve System, and Federal Reserve System to refer collectively to the Federal Reserve Board and the Reserve Banks,

[56] At the time of these authorizations, section 13(3) allowed the Federal Reserve Board, in "unusual and exigent circumstances," to authorize any Reserve Bank to extend credit in the form of a discount to individuals, partnerships, or corporations when the credit was indorsed or otherwise secured to the satisfaction of the Reserve Bank, after obtaining evidence that the individual, partnership, or corporation was unable to secure adequate credit accommodations from other banking institutions. As a result of amendments to section 13(3) made by the Dodd-Frank Wall Street Reform and Consumer Protection Act (Pub. L. No. 111-203), the Federal Reserve Board can now authorize 13(3) lending only through programs or facilities with broad-based eligibility.

[57] Mortgage-backed securities are securities that represent claims to the cash flows from pools of mortgage loans, such as mortgages on residential property.

[58] The sudden spike in the cost of term funding followed the August 9, 2007, announcement by BNP Paribas, a large banking organization based in France, that it could not value certain mortgage-related assets in three of its investment funds because of a lack of liquidity in U.S. securitization markets. Greater reliance on overnight borrowing increased the volatility of banks' funding costs and increased "roll-over" risk, or the risk that banks would not be able to renew their funding as loans matured.

[59] One basis point is equivalent to 0.01 percent or 1/100th of a percent.

[60] Federal Reserve Board, *Monetary Policy Report to the Congress* (February 27, 2008). Available at http://www.federalreserve.gov/boarddocs/hh/2008/february/fullreport.pdf. This paper observed that the average interest rate in interbank lending markets was almost equal, on average, to the lower discount rate. In addition, because of the perceived stigma associated with borrowing from the discount window, depository institutions may have been reluctant to turn to the discount window for funding support.

[61] Section 10B of the Federal Reserve Act provides the Reserve Banks broad authority to extend credit to depository institutions.

[62] Another important advantage of TAF relative to encouraging greater use of the discount window was that the Federal Reserve Board could more easily control the impact of auctioned funds on monetary policy. While the Federal Reserve Board could not predict with certainty the demand for discount window loans, it could control the amount of TAF loans provided at each auction. As a result, the FOMC and FRBNY could more easily coordinate monetary policy operations to offset the impact of TAF auctions. For example, to offset the injection of $75 billion of reserves into the financial system in the form of TAF loans, FRBNY could sell $75 billion of Treasury securities through its open market operations. All else equal, the net effect of these two actions would be to have no impact on total reserves.

[63] When TAF auction demand was less than the total amount offered for the TAF auction, the interest rate resulting from the auction was the minimum bid rate set by the Federal Reserve Board—not a competitively determined rated.

[64] For example, an FRBNY staff paper observed that by facilitating access to dollar funding the swap lines could reduce the need for foreign banks to sell dollar assets into stressed markets, which could have further reduced prices for these dollar assets.

[65] The Federal Reserve Board has interpreted section 14 of the Federal Reserve Act to permit the Federal Reserve Banks to conduct open market operations in foreign exchange markets and to open and maintain accounts in foreign currency with foreign central banks. Section 14 states that "[a]ny Federal reserve bank may... purchase and sell in the open market, at home or abroad, either from or to domestic or foreign banks, firms, corporations, or individuals, cable transfers..." The Federal Reserve Board has interpreted "cable transfers" to mean foreign exchange. Section 14(e) authorizes Reserve Banks to "open and maintain accounts in foreign countries, appoint correspondents, and establish agencies in such countries..." and "to open and maintain banking accounts for... foreign banks or bankers...." The use of swap lines under section 14 of the Federal Reserve Act is not new. For example, FRBNY instituted temporary swap arrangements following September 11, 2001, with the European Central Bank and the Bank of England.

[66] These foreign central banks were the Reserve Bank of Australia, the Banco Central do Brasil, the Bank of Canada, Danmarks Nationalbank (Denmark), the Bank of England (United Kingdom), the Bank of Japan, the Bank of Korea (South Korea), the Banco de Mexico, the Reserve Bank of New Zealand, Norges Bank (Norway), the Monetary Authority of Singapore, and Sveriges Riksbank (Sweden).

[67] When the market value of assets used to secure or collateralize repurchase transactions declines, borrowers are usually required to post additional collateral.

[68] Unusually high demand for certain U.S. Treasury securities resulted in negative yields on these securities at times during the crisis, indicating that investors were willing to accept a small loss in return for the relative safety of these securities.

[69] For more information about the potential causes and impacts of downward price spirals, see GAO, *Financial Markets Regulation: Financial Crisis Highlights Need to Improve Oversight of Leverage at Financial Institutions and across System*, GAO-09-739 (Washington, D.C.: July 22, 2009).

[70] Before the crisis, FRBNY ran an overnight securities lending facility, the terms of which involved the lending of certain Treasury securities by FRBNY to primary dealers against other Treasury securities as collateral. Certain of the legal infrastructure for the traditional securities lending program was used for TSLF. Other legal and operational infrastructure had to be created specifically for TSLF.

[71] TSLF held separate auctions of Treasury securities against two different schedules of collateral to better calibrate the interest rate on TSLF loans to the level of risk associated with the collateral. The Federal Reserve Board set a higher minimum interest rate for schedule 2 TSLF auctions, which accepted riskier collateral types than schedule 1 auctions.

[72] Bear Stearns was one of the largest primary dealers and engaged in a broad range of activities, including investment banking, securities and derivatives trading, brokerage services, and origination and securitization of mortgage loans.

[73] In our prior work on the financial crisis, Securities and Exchange Commission officials told us that neither they nor the broader regulatory community anticipated this development and that the Securities and Exchange Commission had not directed large broker-dealer holding companies to plan for the unavailability of secured funding in their contingent funding plans. Securities and Exchange Commission officials stated that no financial institution could survive without secured funding. Rumors about clients moving cash and security balances elsewhere and, more importantly, counterparties not transacting with Bear Stearns also placed strains on the firm's ability to obtain secured financing. See GAO-09-739.

[74] The loan was made through JP Morgan Chase Bank, National Association pursuant to FRBNY's discount window authority under section 1 0B of the Federal Reserve Act. Recognizing that the ultimate borrower was Bear Stearns, a nondepository institution, the Board of Governors voted on the afternoon of March 14, 2008, to authorize the loan under

section 13(3) authority. Federal Reserve Board officials explained that the use of JP Morgan Chase Bank, National Association as an intermediary was not strictly required as section 13(3) permitted a direct loan to Bear Stearns. However, they used the back-to- back loan structure because this was the structure FRBNY lawyers had prepared for in developing required legal documentation late on Thursday, March 13, 2008.

[75] Timothy F. Geithner, testimony before the U.S. Senate Committee on Banking, Housing and Urban Affairs (Washington, D.C., Apr. 3, 2008).

[76] Under the terms outlined in this letter and approved by the Federal Reserve Board, FRBNY agreed to lend up to $30 billion to JPMC against eligible Bear Stearns collateral listed in an attachment to the letter. The types and amounts of eligible collateral under this agreement were broadly similar to the assets ultimately included under the final lending structure, Maiden Lane LLC. The agreed price of the collateral was to be based on Bear Stearns's valuation of the collateral as of March 14, 2008, regardless of the date of any lending to JPMC under this agreement. JPMC would not have been required to post margin in any amount to secure any borrowing under this agreement. The letter also included certain regulatory exemptions for JPMC in connection with its agreement to acquire Bear Stearns. For example, the Federal Reserve Board granted an 18-month exemption to JPMC from the Federal Reserve Board's risk-based and leverage capital requirements for bank holding companies. The exemption would allow JPMC to exclude the assets and exposures of Bear Stearns from its risk-weighted assets for purposes of applying the risk-based capital requirements at the parent bank holding company.

[77] Before the crisis, FRBNY regularly undertook traditional temporary open market operations—repurchase agreement transactions—with primary dealers. The repurchase transactions, in normal times, are used by FRBNY to attempt to meet the target federal funds rate, as directed by the FOMC, by temporarily increasing the amount of reserves. The repurchase transactions undertaken pursuant to PDCF were not for the purpose of increasing reserves (although they did do that), but rather for extending credit as authorized by the Federal Reserve Board.

[78] For TSLF, previously, only Treasury securities, agency securities, and AAA-rated mortgage-backed and asset-backed securities could be pledged. For PDCF, previously, eligible collateral had to have at least an investment-grade rating. Tri-party repurchase agreements include three parties: the borrower, the lender, and a tri-party agent that facilitates the repurchase agreement transaction by providing custody of the securities posted as collateral and valuing the collateral, among other services.

[79] Concurrently, the Federal Reserve Board announced that it had approved applications by Goldman Sachs and Morgan Stanley to become bank holding companies. In addition, Bank of America agreed to acquire Merrill Lynch, which would become part of a bank holding company pending completion of its merger with Bank of America, a bank holding company supervised by the Federal Reserve System. On November 23, 2008, in connection with other actions taken by Treasury, FDIC, and the Federal Reserve Board to assist Citigroup Inc., the Federal Reserve Board authorized FRBNY to extend credit to the London-based broker-dealer of Citigroup on terms similar to those applicable to PDCF loans. The other actions taken to assist Citigroup Inc. are discussed later in this appendix.

[80] A mutual fund is a company that pools money from many investors and invests the money in stocks, bonds, short-term money market instruments, other securities or assets, or some combination of these investments. These investments constitute the fund's portfolio. Mutual funds are registered and regulated under the Investment Company Act of 1940, and are supervised by the Securities and Exchange Commission. Mutual funds sell shares to public investors. Each share represents an investor's proportionate ownership in the fund's holdings and the income those holdings generate. Mutual fund shares are "redeemable," which means that when mutual fund investors want to sell their shares, the investors sell them back to the fund, or to a broker acting for the fund, at their current net asset value per share, minus any fees the fund may charge. MMMFs are mutual funds that are registered

under the Investment Company Act of 1940, and regulated under Securities and Exchange Commission rule 2a-7 under that act. MMMFs invest in high- quality, short-term debt instruments such as commercial paper, treasury bills, and repurchase agreements. Generally, these funds, unlike other investment companies, seek to maintain a stable net asset value per share (market value of assets minus liabilities divided by number of shares outstanding), typically $1 per share.

[81] Many financial institutions created ABCP conduits that would purchase various assets, including mortgage-related securities, financial institution debt, and receivables from industrial businesses. To obtain funds to purchase these assets, these conduits borrowed using shorter-term debt instruments, such as ABCP and medium-term notes. The difference between the interest paid to the ABCP or note holders and the income earned on the entity's assets produced fee and other income for the sponsoring institution. However, these structures carried the risk that the entity would find it difficult or costly to renew its debt financing under less-favorable market conditions.

[82] A branch or agency of a foreign bank is a legal extension of the foreign bank and is not a freestanding entity in the United States. Foreign bank branches and agencies operating in the United States are subject to Federal Reserve regulations, and the Federal Reserve examines most foreign bank branches and agencies annually.

[83] There are two main types of commercial paper: unsecured and asset-backed. Unsecured paper is not backed by collateral, and the credit rating of the issuing institution is a key variable in determining the cost of its issuance. In contrast, ABCP is collateralized by assets and therefore is a secured form of borrowing.

[84] The CPFF SPV was needed to allow FRBNY to engage in market transactions (purchases of commercial paper) outside its traditional operating framework for discount window lending.

[85] Commercial paper generally has fixed maturities of 1 to 270 days.

[86] Securitization is a process by which similar debt instruments—such as loans, leases, or receivables—are aggregated into pools, and interest-bearing securities backed by such pools are then sold to investors. These asset-backed securities provide a source of liquidity for consumers and small businesses because financial institutions can take assets that they would otherwise hold on their balance sheets, sell them as securities, and use the proceeds to originate new loans, among other purposes.

[87] Initially, securities backed by automobile, credit card, student loans, and loans guaranteed by the Small Business Administration were deemed eligible for TALF because of the need to make credit in these sectors more widely available. The Federal Reserve Board later expanded TALF-eligibility to other ABS classes, including commercial mortgage-backed securities.

[88] TALF loans were made without recourse to the intermediary borrower. However, under the TALF lending agreement, if FRBNY found that the collateral provided for a TALF loan or a borrower who had participated in the program was found to be ineligible, the nonrecourse feature of the loan would become inapplicable.

[89] Through AIGFP—a financial products subsidiary that engaged in a variety of financial transactions, including standard and customized financial products—AIG was a participant in the derivatives market. The securities lending program allowed insurance companies, primarily life insurance companies, to lend securities in return for cash collateral that was invested in residential mortgage-backed securities.

[90] Credit default swaps are bilateral contracts that are sold over the counter and transfer credit risks from one party to another. The seller, who is offering credit protection, agrees, in return for a periodic fee, to compensate the buyer if a specified credit event, such as default, occurs. Collateralized debt obligations are securities backed by a pool of bonds, loans, or other assets.

[91] All three Maiden Lane SPVs incorporated a first-loss position for the private sector that was equal to the difference between the total purchase price of the assets and the amount of the FRBNY loan.

[92] On January 14, 2011, using proceeds from the initial public offering of AIA Group Limited and the sale of American Life Insurance Company to another insurance company, AIG repaid its outstanding balance on the AIG RCF.

[93] See also GAO, *Troubled Asset Relief Program: Status of Government Assistance Provided to AIG,* GAO-09-975 (Washington, D.C.: Sept. 21, 2009).

[94] As of September 30, 2008, Citigroup was the second largest banking organization in the United States, with total consolidated assets of approximately $2 trillion. Citigroup was and remains a major supplier of credit and one of the largest deposit holders in the United States and the world.

[95] For more information about the basis for the federal government's assistance to Citigroup, see GAO-10-100.

[96] The amount of this "attachment point" for FRBNY was approximately $56.17 billion. Even in stress scenarios, FRBNY did not expect losses to reach this level.

[97] Although FRBNY did not lend to Citigroup under this lending commitment, FRBNY staff confirmed that Citigroup subsidiaries were permitted under the agreement to pledge ring-fence assets as collateral to the Federal Reserve Board's emergency loan programs, such as PDCF, TSLF, and TAF, subject to the terms and conditions for these programs. The Citigroup loss sharing agreement was clear, however, that if FRBNY ever were to lend to Citigroup under the agreement, all such pledges would need to be removed.

[98] In June and December 2009, the House of Representatives Subcommittee on Domestic Policy, Committee on Government Oversight and Reform, held hearings on the events that led to federal government assistance to protect Bank of America against losses from Merrill Lynch assets. Committee members expressed concerns about the reasons for this intervention when Bank of America had already agreed to acquire Merrill Lynch without government assistance.

[99] Agency MBS include MBS issued by the housing government-sponsored enterprises, which are Fannie Mae and Freddie Mac, or guaranteed by Ginnie Mae.

[100] Three Reserve Banks had a vacant director position at some time during 2010, reducing the total number of directors who served the full year during 2010 from 108 to 105.

In: The Federal Reserve ISBN: 978-1-62081-034-7
Editors: G. R. Conley and A. A. Sanford© 2012 Nova Science Publishers, Inc.

Chapter 3

AUDIT THE FED HEARING — AUERBACH TESTIMONY*

Robert D. Auerbach

INTRODUCTION

Thank you Chairman Ron Paul, Ranking Member William Lacy Clay and members of the subcommittee for this opportunity to testify on transparency at the Federal Reserve. My name is Robert Auerbach. I am a Professor of Public Policy at the Lyndon B. Johnson School of Public Affairs at the University of Texas in Austin. On two separate occasions I had the honor to serve as an economist on the staff of this committee (1977-81 and 1992-1997) and my 2008 book, Deception and Abuse at the Fed: Henry B. Gonzalez Battles Alan Greenspan"s Bank details the oversight investigations that I staffed while serving Committee Chairman Henry S. Reuss in the late 1970's and Committee Chairman/Ranking Member Henry B. Gonzalez in the 1990's. I have also served as an economist in the U.S. Treasury's Office of Domestic Monetary Affairs during the Reagan administration and at the Federal Reserve System.

* This is an edited, reformatted and augmented version of the "Audit the Fed: Dodd-Frank, QE 3, and Federal Reserve Transparency", Lyndon Baines Johnson School of Public Affairs, University of Texas at Austin before the Subcommittee on Domestic Monetary Policy and Technology Committee on Financial Services U.S. House of Representatives, dated October 4, 2011.

The Fed is the powerful central bank of the United States that controls the money supply, regulates the banking system and, since 1962, makes loans to foreign countries without Congressional authorization. [1] The historical record summarized below, describing Federal Reserve officials blocking transparency and individual accountability, including destroying source records of its policymaking committee since 1995, leads to the following suggested remedies:

- **Independent Inspector General:** The Inspector General of the Federal Reserve should not be appointed by the chairman of the Federal Reserve Board as is currently the case. The IG should be a Presidential nominee whose credentials, abilities and independence are examined during a Senate confirmation process.
- **Preserve Transcripts:** The Federal Reserve should stop destroying the source transcripts and should stop turning off the recording system at its policy making committee, the Federal Open Market Committee (FOMC). This practice was approved in 1995 by an unrecorded vote of the FOMC directed by then-Chairman Alan Greenspan.[2]
- **Provide Minutes to Congress:** The minutes of the boards of directors meetings at the Federal Reserve"s 12 district banks and the transcripts of the meetings of the Federal Reserve Board of Governors and of the FOMC, should be sent to the House and Senate banking committees within six months of the meetings. Trained archivists at the National Archives and Records Administration should edit those records to remove prescribed items in cooperation with the Federal Reserve.
- **Senate Confirmation of Bank Presidents:** The 12 Federal Reserve regional bank presidents who are eligible to vote on the money supply as members of the FOMC should be confirmed by the Senate. The presidents wield enormous power as members of the FOMC and they should be fully vetted in the confirmation process. I want to commend full committee Ranking Member Barnie Frank for addressing the regional bank presidents" role on the FOMC with H.R. 1512, although rather than removing them from the FOMC as proposed in the bill I would recommend Senate confirmation.

FED AUDITS

Chairman Ron Paul and Senator Bernie Sanders deserve great praise for their leadership in enacting the current Government Accountability Office (GAO) audit of the Federal Reserve as part of the Dodd-Frank Act. The Senate unanimously approved, by a 90 to 0 vote, the Sanders amendment to require disclosure of the recipients of the Fed's emergency loans. Hopefully this Congressional action set a precedent for fuller continuing audits of Federal Reserve operations.

In 1976, House Committee on Banking, Finance and Urban Affairs Chairman Henry Reuss proposed a GAO audit of the Fed. The Fed orchestrated a massive lobbying campaign using the officials of private banks to lobby to stop the audit bill.

Evidence of the lobbying campaign came from minutes of the board of directors of each of the 12 district Federal Reserve Banks. Chairman Reuss requested minutes from district bank meetings from 1972, 1974, and 1975. After a six-month delay with letters back and forth and meetings between Chairman Reuss and Federal Reserve Chairman Arthur Burns, the minutes arrived at the Congress. One response to the Reuss request for records was given by a St. Louis Fed president, as reported on the transcript:

> "I would also think that if this involves a lot of work, which it will, needless work, that someone on Mr. Reuss" Committee, a friendly individual should know what we"re being called upon to do. Because I think this can be used against Reuss if we react intelligently and as I see it in the St. Louis case, it"s appalling how skimpy or meaningless our minutes are, I"m sure we did this with great wisdom knowing that a man named Reuss would ask for them. The minutes are really terribly shallow. Tell nothing."[3] (Emphasis added)

Chairman Reuss" delivered a floor speech in 1976 detailing the evidence of the Fed"s orchestrated lobby against the audit bill entitled: "What the Secret Minutes of the Federal Reserve Banks Meetings Disclose". The speech led to the passage of the Federal Reserve Reform Act of 1977 which brought Fed Bank directors under the federal government conflict of interest laws.

Despite this victory, the Fed won the first round on the audit effort. Chairman Reuss"s audit bill could not garner enough support to pass out of the Committee. It was shunted to the Government Operations Committee where it passed in 1978, but only after glaring no-audit barriers on any Fed operations connected to monetary policy or international transactions were added.

In the Fed's monetary policy operations billions of dollars can be made from inside information from leaks of Fed policy. It is very difficult to police these leaks of inside information. One necessary step to stop leaks is to severely limit the interest rate policy information in the Federal Reserve to a few people. This has not happened. Many hundreds of Federal Reserve employees -- over 500 employees -- are directly involved in the secret meetings or in preparing information that has been discussed at these meetings.

The House Banking Committee received information in 1997 about non-Federal Reserve employees at Federal Reserve meetings where inside information was discussed. Congressmen Gonzalez and Maurice Hinchey asked Greenspan about the apparent leak of discount rate information and the presence of these people at Federal Reserve meetings. Greenspan was forced to admit that some non-Federal Reserve people had attended Federal Reserve meetings where the Federal Reserve=s future interest rate policy was discussed.[4] Greenspan included a 23-page enclosure listing hundreds of people at the Board of Governors in Washington, D.C. and in the 12 Federal Reserve Banks around the country who have access to at least some secret Federal Reserve information about non-public Federal Reserve interest rate policy.

Names of Avisiting scholars@ were listed who had attended pre-FOMC meetings at three Federal Reserve Banks. Greenspan also wrote:

> At the Federal Reserve Bank of Kansas City, over the 3-year period, a total of 28 foreign central bankers have attended 16 different Board of Directors meetings, including the discussion and vote on discount rates. Those attending included Acentral bankers from Bulgaria, China, the Czech Republic, Hungry, Poland, Romania and Russia.[5]

At the December 19, 1989 FOMC meeting Greenspan warned about the ill effects of continuing leaks from the FOMC"s supposedly secret meetings and said that "we're beginning to look like buffoons":

> [. . .] I would like to raise again a problem that continues to confront this organization with continuous damaging and corrosive effects, and that is the

issue of leaks out of this Committee. We have two extraordinary leaks, and perhaps more, in recent days: in which John Berry at The Washington Post in late November had the time and content of a telephone conference; previous to that we had The Wall Street Journal knowing about telephone conferences and knowing a number of things that could only have come out of this Committee.

As best I can judge from feedback I"m getting from friends of ours the credibility of this organization is beginning to recede and we're beginning to look like buffoons to some of them. [. . .] [6]

FOMC Records

In 1976 two threats to Fed secrecy created high anxiety at the Federal Reserve Board of Governors. First, David Merrill, a law student at Georgetown University, brought a legal action challenging the 45-day delay in releasing the "Directive" on monetary policy.[7] It is a short report on policy actions that were authorized at the FOMC meeting. The Federal District Court agreed with Merrill. The Fed appealed up to the Supreme Court which remanded it back to the district court. Lacking funds for further extensive adjudication Merrill could not pursue the case. The Fed has all the money it needs or can order from the Bureau of Engraving and Printing to hire private law firms and fight any legal action.

The second attack on the Fed"s secrecy was Congressional consideration of the "Government in the Sunshine Act" that was signed into law September 13, 1976. That law required that: "The agency shall make promptly available to the public, in a place easily accessible to the public, the transcript, electronic recording or minutes of the meeting." The Fed frantically tried to protect itself from such transparency and individual accountability. Fearing the new legislation and the pending legal action for the disclosure of their records, Federal Reserve Chairman Arthur Burns led the Federal Reserve Open Market Committee in a 10 to 1 vote to discontinue transcripts of its meetings in 1976. That vote began the official 17- year Fed lie asserting that no transcripts were being maintained of FOMC meetings.

In 1992 I returned to the Banking Committee staff of then-Chairman Henry B. Gonzalez. Chairman Gonzalez and I could not believe that the most powerful central bank in the world, operating in our great democracy, had no complete records of its policy making committee, the FOMC. On October 19, 1993, Chairman Gonzalez convened a Fed oversight hearing focusing on transcripts. Seventeen officials of the Fed, seven members of the Board of Governors and ten of the twelve presidents of the Federal Reserve District Banks, testified in the Banking Committee chamber. Chairman Greenspan sat in the center of the long row of Fed officials. Prior to the hearing, Chairman Gonzalez sent the witnesses specific instructions that they reveal details of what records are kept by the Fed of their meetings.

A top Fed staff person, who would become vice chairman of the Board of Governors, explained on a confidential FOMC conference call four days before their Congressional testimony that Greenspan clearly intended to mislead Congress about written records of the FOMC: "The Chairman is not highlighting these transcripts ...We're not waving red flags." [8]

Jim McTague, now the Washington editor of Barron"s, wrote about Greenspan's testimony: "In a performance that would have made professor Irwin Corey weep with admiration Mr. Greenspan avoided drawing attention to the existence of transcripts ..." Corey famously performed as a double-talking comedian.[9]

Several days after the hearing, the Cleveland Fed broke the silence and misdirection and informed the Congress of the deception. Chairman Greenspan then sent a letter admitting that transcripts existed. He claimed to have had memory problems. I led a group of Republican and Democratic staff to the Board of Governors where Fed staff showed us 17 years of neatly typed transcripts around the corner from Chairman Greenspan's office. Under pressure from this Gonzalez investigation the Fed ended its 17-year lie by again issuing the transcripts but only with a 5-year lag, too long to establish timely individual accountability.

In 1995 Greenspan held a non-recorded vote of the FOMC – no finger prints – to destroy the source FOMC transcripts. I was informed by the Fed Vice Chairman Donald Kohn that this destruction would continue and that it was legal.[10] Previously these source records had been sent to the National Archives.

That same year the shredding machines at the Fed destroyed the source FOMC records when Fed officials bypassed the Congress and voted $5 billion to support the Mexican peso. That loan was collateralized by revenue from Mexico"s oil industry. When the loan authorization was sent to the New York Federal Reserve Bank and was public information the peso stopped falling. The loan to Mexico that had been authorized was then not needed and was not made.

INVESTIGATIONS OF FED OPERATIONS

Congresswoman Carolyn Maloney joined Chairman Gonzalez in an investigation from 1995 to 1997 of the Fed"s more than 50 contracted airplanes that were delivering paper checks across the country. The investigation found evidence of corruption in this system typified by the "backup plane" at Teterboro Airport. The Fed paid for this contracted plane that people at that Fed facility called the phantom plane because it was not present at Teterboro much of the time. We also uncovered evidence of nearly nonexistent in-house audits. Officials covered losses in the airplane fleet operations by transferring money from the Fed's employee pension fund.

The Reno Justice Department refused the Gonzalez request to investigate the extensive corruption found in the management of the airplane fleet and referred the Gonzalez inquiry to the Fed"s Inspector General. The IG told me he did not know if he had jurisdiction because the fleet was managed by the Boston regional Fed Bank.

That weak dodge is consistent with my prior experience and underlies the importance of changing the structure of the Fed"s IG. The Fed's Report to Congress and the Dodd-Frank law grant the Chairman of the Federal Reserve the authority to appoint his own Inspector General who is charged with investigating the Fed bureaucracy and who also serves as the IG for the new Consumer Financial Protection Bureau. This is a clear conflict as Chairman Bernanke can "prohibit the Fed's Inspector General from carrying out or completing an audit or investigation or from issuing a subpoena ...": [11]

Another Gonzalez investigation began in 1997 when the Congress received information about alleged corrupt accounting at the cash section of the Los Angeles branch of the San Francisco Federal Reserve Bank that includes vaults containing cash and coins. The GAO assisted the Gonzalez's investigation. During the investigation Chairman Greenspan informed Ranking Member Gonzalez that the Federal Reserve knew that nearly $500 thousand that had been stolen from Fed vaults by Fed employees from 1987 to 1996.[12] The Gonzalez/GAO investigation indicated this was an understatement.

The following selections are from the September 30, 1996 published report of an excellent GAO team that investigated the cash section at the Los Angeles Branch of the Federal Reserve in coordination with a Gonzalez investigation. The report indicates how desperately the Fed operations need a complete competent audit. It is a matter of national security:

A bank had brought a deposit of $432,000 to the Fed and Fed employees mistakenly entered the transaction as $8,640,000. When Fed employees in the cash department counted the deposit they discovered an $8,208,000 mistake "they overrode the system control in the cash inventory system and forwarded the money for further processing. Although this error was corrected when the problem was detected at the end of the day, this resulted in an erroneous entry being made in the L.A. Bank"s ledger for $8,640,000 that increased the cash in the vault amount and the depository institution"s account. L.A. Bank officials had no explanation for why this occurred."

The GAO also reported: "We found that the October, November, and December 1995 monthly currency activity reports of the L.A. Bank were prepared and reported incorrectly. We confirmed that the reported receipts from currency deposited in the L.A. Bank by depository institutions (receipts from circulation) were not taken from the L.A. Bank"s cash inventory records (in other words, independently determined) but rather "forced" to ensure that the currency activity reports agreed with the daily balance sheet for the last day of the month." "The reports were prepared incorrectly at the direction of the L.A. Bank"s management. L.A. Bank officials stated that the practice of forcing the reports to agree had been in place for some time." "We found that problems in currency reporting are linked to the limitations in the design of the underlying cash inventory system." "The L.A. Bank"s inability to precisely summarize currency activity from its cash inventory records raises serious questions about the integrity of its accounting and internal controls." "We attempted to perform a comprehensive review of the L.A. Bank"s internal controls and accounting practices over the money flowing through the Bank. Our efforts to perform a comprehensive review were substantially limited by the L.A. banks inability to provide the information needed for such a review.[...] we requested that the Bank provide us with [. . .] a general ledger history of all of the activity in its general ledger cash accounts for October through December 1995" [The bank did not provide the] general ledger of cash transactions because Bank officials stated that it would take them 3 weeks." [13]

This excellent GAO report demonstrates that the agency is capable of conducting exemplary audits of Fed operations if it is not constrained by statutory limitations and as long as experienced staff lead the investigations. The Fed vault facilities are a crucial part of the nation"s payment system and should be a national security priority with full accountability to the Congress. The Fed banks contain uncirculated currency and coin transferred from the Bureau of Engraving and Printing. They also receive cash from banks throughout the country. The cash sections and vaults of the Federal Reserve District Banks and branches need to be investigated and audited with personnel who are experienced in central bank operations, independent of Fed officials and instructed to make thorough audits.

ACADEMIC INDEPENDENCE

Future GAO audits should target the massive number of Fed payments to academics who are not employed at the Federal Reserve. A Gonzalez investigation found that the Federal Reserve sent money and provided other benefits to economists throughout academia who specialize in monetary and financial subjects, and who were not employees of the Federal Reserve. The Fed itself employed over 500 economists so the need to make all these outside payments is highly questionable.[14] Some academics received checks from a number of (up to five) district Fed Banks. Reuters reported Milton Friedman's views on this problem in 1993: "the Fed"s relatively enhanced standing among the public has been aided "by the fact the Fed has always paid a great deal of attention to soothing the people in the media and buying up its most likely critics' Recognizing that the Fed employs "probably half of the monetary economists in the U.S. and has visiting appointments for two-thirds of the rest" he [Friedman] saw few among the academic community who were prepared to criticize the Fed policy." [15]

CONCLUSION

The current GAO audit of the Federal Reserve is a historic step towards greater transparency at the central bank. The Fed has a long history of fighting outside audits as various Fed officials have complained that they would constitute an infringement on central bank independence. In fact, the Fed"s mythical flag of independence from politics, a favorite Fed mantra to avoid individual responsibility, is merely a shield intended to protect the institution from being forced to act in a more transparent fashion. Ongoing audits do not infringe on the Fed"s independence which is protected in a myriad of ways, including self-funding and terms for members of the Board of Governors of 14 years. Board of Governor members can only be removed by impeachment and that has never happened.

Their long terms and very little chance of being impeached should allow independent votes. It has not prevented the fact that monetary policy has been very poor in periods such as the 1970"s and since October 2008. I have been writing and speaking about the Federal Reserve"s present misguided policy since 2009.[16]

Complete GAO audits and the other improvements I have described are essential for establishing a timely authentic record of policy actions and individual responsibility for the powerful unelected officials at the nation's central bank.

End Notes

[1] Auerbach, *Deception and Abuse at the Fed*, pp. 69 - 73.

[2] Auerbach, *Deception and Abuse at the Fed*, pp. 103 - 104.

[3] November 16, 1976 FOMC transcript, p.17.

[4] Greenspan letter of April 25, 1997.

[5] Greenspan letter to Chairman Gonzalez, April 25, 1997, p. 2.

[6] Chapter 9, "Valuable Secrets and the Return of Greenspan's "Prophetic Touch" in *Deception and Abuse at the Fed*.

[7] The secret meetings at the Board of Governors in Washington D.C. revealed great alarm about transparency at the Arthur Burns Fed. This response was revealed in the FOMC transcripts Burns left upon his death in 1987 to the President R. Gerald Ford Library on the University of Michigan campus. The archivists of the National Archives and Records Administration lightly edited the transcripts.

[8] FOMC conference call transcript, October 15, 1993, p. 20.

[9] "Greenspan Has Himself to Blame for Fervid Interest in Transcripts," *American Banker*, December 1, 1993, p. 24.

[10] A letter from then Vice Chairman Donald Kohn to Robert Auerbach September 1, 2001. Included in Auerbach, "Stop the Fed From Shredding Its Record," *Huffington Post*, December 9, 2001.

[11] Section 1081 of the Dodd-Frank Wall Street Reform and Consumer Protection Act states that, "...the Chairman of the Board of Governors of the Federal Reserve System shall appoint the Inspector General of the Board of Governors of the Federal Reserve System and the Bureau of Consumer Financial Protection. The Inspector General of the Board of Governors of the Federal Reserve System and the Bureau of Consumer Financial Protection shall have all of the authorities and responsibilities provided by this Act with respect to the Bureau of Consumer Financial Protection, as if the Bureau were part of the Board of Governors of the Federal Reserve System."

[12] Federal Reserve Board of Governors Chairman Alan Greenspan letter to Ranking Member Gonzalez, December 5, 1996.

[13] "*Federal Reserve Banks, Inaccurate Reporting of Currency at the Los Angeles Branch*, "Report to the Ranking Minority Member [The Honorable Henry B. Gonzalez], Committee on Banking and Financial Services," House of Representatives. GAO/AIMD-96-146, September 30, 1996. See also "EMBEZZLING FED MONEY AND FALSIFYING ACCOUNTING RECORDS," *Deception and Abuse* At the Fed," pp. 55-60.

[14] After the chapter in my book, "When 500 economists are not enough," was published on *Huffington Post*, , September 7, 2009, Ryan Grim followed up with an up to date article: "Priceless: How the Fed Bought the Economics Profession," September 7, 2009.

[15] Reuters interview reported July 7, 1993.

[16] "The Bernanke Fed Is in a Deep Hole With a $1.6 Trillion Time Bomb," *Huffington Post/AOL*, August 29, 2011.

In: The Federal Reserve ISBN: 978-1-62081-034-7
Editors: G. R. Conley and A. A. Sanford© 2012 Nova Science Publishers, Inc.

Chapter 4

AUDIT THE FED HEARING — CALABRIA TESTIMONY*

Mark A. Calabria

Chairman Paul, Ranking Member Clay, and distinguished members of the subcommittee, I thank you for the invitation to appear at today's important hearing. I am Mark Calabria, Director of Financial Regulation Studies at the Cato Institute, a nonprofit, non-partisan public policy research institute located here in Washington, DC. Before I begin my testimony, I would like to make clear that my comments are solely my own and do not represent any official policy positions of the Cato Institute. In addition, outside of my interest as a citizen and taxpayer, I have no direct financial interest in the subject matter before the Committee today, nor do I represent any entities that do.

THE FEDERAL RESERVE AND THE FINANCIAL CRISIS

As the subcommittee is well aware, the events of 2008 witnessed not only unprecedented disruptions to our financial markets, but also extraordinary responses on the part of our financial regulators and central bank. No entity

* This is an edited, reformatted and augmented version of the Committee on Financial Services Subcommittee on Domestic Monetary Policy and Technology On "Audit the Fed: Dodd-Frank, QE3, and Federal Reserve Transparency", U.S. House of Representatives, dated October 4, 2011.

was more deeply involved than the Federal Reserve System ("Fed"), particularly the Federal Reserve Bank of New York.

Yet the Fed has consistently and repeated resisted efforts to bring any accountability and transparency to its actions. Congress and the public were regularly warned that if the details of the Fed's actions became public, further panic would ensue in our financial markets. For instance I distinctly remember, as a staffer for the Senate Banking Committee, listening to then Fed Vice Chair Donald Kohn tell that Committee that making the names of AIG's derivatives counterparties public would severely harm our financial markets. When those names were eventually released our world did not come to an end. In short, the Fed has a long tradition and strong preference for secrecy. Despite some notable attempts by the Fed to increase its communications with the public, I believe, given its track record, the public cannot rely on the Fed to voluntarily provide us with sufficient information to monitor its activities and judge the effectiveness of its actions. And while the requirements of the Dodd-Frank Wall Street Reform and Consumer Protection Act ("Dodd-Frank"), in relation to auditing the Fed's activities are an important advance, they fall far too short of providing sufficient oversight of the Fed.

What auditing has been conducted has so far been focused on the Fed's response to the crisis. Among economists, on both the right and the left, there remains considerable concern and debate over the Fed's role in helping to create the crisis via its easy money policies in the aftermath of the dotcom bubble and the events of 9/11. If we truly wish to end financial crises, then I believe it is absolutely essential that Congress receive a full and objective evaluation of the Fed's role in fostering the housing bubble, particularly as it relates to monetary policy decisions made between 2002 and 2005.

FEDERAL RESERVE AUDIT REQUIREMENTS UNDER DODD-FRANK

The primary audit requirements of Dodd-Frank, as they relate to the Fed's actions during the financial crisis, are contained in Section 1109, which directs GAO to:

> "**conduct a onetime audit** of all loans and other financial assistance provided during the period beginning on December 1, 2007 and ending on the date of enactment of this Act by the Board of Governors or a Federal reserve

> bank under the Asset-Backed Commercial Paper Money Market Mutual Fund Liquidity Facility, the Term Asset-Backed Securities Loan Facility, the Primary Dealer Credit Facility, the Commercial Paper Funding Facility, the Term Securities Lending Facility, the Term Auction Facility, Maiden Lane, Maiden Lane II, Maiden Lane III, the agency Mortgage- Backed Securities program, foreign currency liquidity swap lines, and any other program created as a result of section 13(3) of the Federal Reserve Act."

That audit was delivered to Congress in July. Importantly, the audit required by Dodd-Frank goes beyond a simple accounting of what was lent to whom, but also requires GAO to evaluate the effectiveness and policies of the various lending facilities. As GAO's audit makes clear, the Fed, and in particular the New York Fed, exercised considerable discretion in designing these lending programs and often did so in an extremely ad hoc manner. While it does appear that the Fed made attempts to treat all program participants fairly and equally, a lack of appropriate internal controls within these programs left open considerable potential for abuse.

In addition to the audit requirements of Section 1109, Dodd-Frank also requires under Section 1103(b) that the Fed provide:

> "disclosure in a timely manner consistent with the purposes of this Act of information concerning the borrowers and counterparties participating in emergency credit facilities, discount window lending programs, and open market operations authorized or conducted by the Board or a Federal reserve bank..."

The importance of Section 1103(b) is that participants in future discount window lending will eventually be identified to the public, along with the terms of such lending. Given that Dodd-Frank gives the Fed approximately two years to disclose such information in relation to discount window lending, I believe the risk that such disclosure will dissuade financial institutions from the use of the discount window has been minimized. Of course, if such disclosure encourages financial institutions to manage their operations in such a way to avoid the need for access to the discount window, then the strength of our financial system would likely be improved.

While Sections 1102, 1103 and 1109 of Dodd-Frank are without doubt improvements in Federal Reserve transparency, and some of the few positive provisions in the Act, they fall short of truly bringing the operations of the Fed into the light of day.

Although I believe it to be a grave mistake to continue to entrust the Federal Reserve with bank supervision and regulation, Congress has chosen to maintain, and extend, that situation. The requirements of Section 1108(b) of Dodd-Frank requiring the Fed's Vice Chair for Supervision to regularly appear before Congress should increase transparency and improve Congressional oversight as it relates to the Fed's bank supervision responsibilities.

THE FEDERAL RESERVE NEEDS A FULL AND CONTINUOUS AUDIT

The non-monetary actions of the Federal Reserve in 2008 and 2009 will likely be debated for decades among economists and historians. Just as the causes of the Great Depression and the effectiveness of the New Deal remain in contention, so will recent actions. What we all can perhaps agree on, or at least hope, is that the extraordinary measures, by Congress, the Federal Reserve and the Treasury, will not be repeated soon or repeated often. Accordingly, much of the audit requirements in Dodd-Frank have something of an "historical" feel to them. However, it is not enough to just get history right, but also to insure that future mistakes are avoided. I can think of few areas requiring as much mistake-avoidance as monetary policy.

Others have already laid out the case that easy money contributed to the crisis,[1] so I will not repeat that argument here. I do believe, however, that the role of easy money in the fostering a housing bubble demonstrates the need for an on-going GAO audit of the Federal Reserve's monetary functions. Disagreement as to the appropriate stance of current monetary policy also demonstrates the need for objective, independent analysis.

WHAT'S GAO FOR?

GAO, the U.S. Government Accountability Office, states its mission is "to support the Congress in meeting its constitutional responsibilities and to help improve the performance and ensure the accountability of the federal government for the benefit of the American people. We provide Congress with timely information that is objective, fact-based, nonpartisan, nonideological, fair, and balanced." (www. gao. gov).

Quite simply GAO is not a political organization. As someone who has interacted repeatedly and regularly with GAO over the last decade, including serving as a Congressional staff liaison for requested GAO reports, I can say they are independent, unbiased and non-political. I have not always agreed with the conclusions of GAO, but I have never felt as if such disagreements were the result of politics or bias.

Subjecting the Federal Reserve's monetary policy function to a GAO audit does not subject the Fed to "politics" – such a claim is not only insulting to GAO, it is insulting to the very concept of Congressional oversight. GAO exists for the very simple reason that no one member of Congress, or their staff, fully understand and are knowledgeable about the functioning of the various government agencies. GAO exists to inform. And there are few areas less understood by Congress than monetary policy and macroeconomics. Hence there are few areas more in need of a GAO audit than the Fed. While the impact of getting wheat support prices or fair market rents wrong is not insignificant, getting monetary policy wrong can be disastrous for an economy.

On Fed Independence

A common objection to a GAO audit of the Fed is that such would "compromise' the Fed's independence and subject its actions to political influence. Such an objection confuses the very nature of Fed independence. The Fed's authority to regulate the value of money is one delegated from Congress. As Congress can, and has, legislated changes to the Fed, it should be clear beyond a doubt that the Fed is not "independent" of Congress. It is a creature of Congress.

Setting aside the debate over the desirability and legitimacy of so-called independent agencies, it should be clear that their independence, in an operational sense, is from the Executive Branch. It should also be clear, however, that in recent years the Fed has coordinated its actions quite closely with the Treasury Department, eroding any real independence. The revolving door, both at the political and career levels, between the Fed and the Treasury departments further undermines the Fed's operational independence. A GAO audit could shine a light on this relationship, helping to insulate the Fed from continued interference by the Treasury Department.

Improving Federal Reserve Transparency

The Dodd-Frank Act made important advances in bringing transparency and accountability to the Federal Reserve. Unfortunately it falls short in allowing Congress, and the public, to truly gauge the effectiveness of the Federal Reserve.

In order to improve Federal Reserve Transparency, Congress should mandate a regular GAO audit of all Fed activities, including monetary policy. Such audits can be performed in such a manner so as to minimize their disruptions to any on-going deliberations of the Federal Open Market Committee (FOMC). For instance audits can be kept confidential for a year after each FOMC meeting.

Evaluating the effectiveness of any government agency is made all the more difficult when that agency faces a variety of competing and sometimes conflicting objectives. If the Fed feels it is free to abandon price stability in order to achieve other objectives, such as supporting the financial industry or misguided attempts to influence the labor market, then an audit will have limited value. At a minimum Congress should restrict the Federal Reserve to a single goal, that of price stability. Congress should also restrict the Fed's discretion in implementing that goal. A central bank that is free to define price stability as whatever it wants is a central bank without any meaningful constraint.

Chairman Paul, Ranking Member Clay and members of the subcommittee, I again thank you for the invitation to appear at today's important hearing. I firmly believe our monetary system was a central driver of the financial crisis and that its deep flaws remain in place. In order to both prevent future financial crises and protect our society from the significant harm that results from inflation, a vigorous debate as to the performance of the Federal Reserve is long overdue.

End Notes

1 See John Taylor, ***Getting Off Track***. Hoover Institute Press. 2009.

INDEX

C

I

J

L

M

N

O

P

I

J

L

M

Q

R

S

T

U

V

W